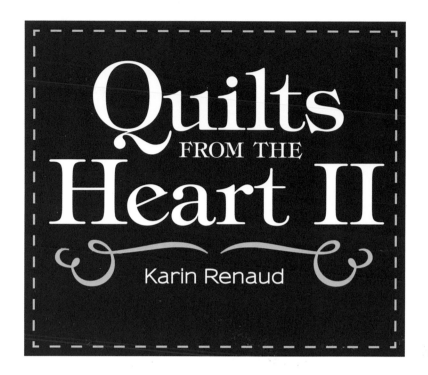

Quilts
FROM THE
Heart II

Karin Renaud

Martingale®
& COMPANY

Quilts from the Heart II
© 2009 by Karin Renaud

& COMPANY

That Patchwork Place® is an imprint of
Martingale & Company®.

Martingale & Company
20205 144th Ave. NE
Woodinville, WA 98072-8478 USA
www.martingale-pub.com

Credits

President & CEO: Tom Wierzbicki
Editorial Director: Mary V. Green
Managing Editor: Tina Cook
Developental Editor: Karen Costello Soltys
Technical Editor: Ellen Pahl
Copy Editor: Marcy Heffernan
Design Director: Stan Green
Production Manager: Regina Girard
Illustrator: Adrienne Smitke
Cover & Text Designer: Adrienne Smitke
Photographer: Brent Kane

Dedication

For Matt, who inspires my creativity,
applauds my efforts, challenges me to grow,
and is always there for me

Printed in China
13 12 11 10 09 08   8 7 6 5 4 3 2 1

Library of Congress Cataloging-in-Publication Data
Library of Congress Control Number: 2008037519

ISBN: 978-1-56477-850-5

Mission Statement

Dedicated to providing quality products
and service to inspire creativity.

Contents

Introduction

When I think about quilting, I think about the nuts and bolts of making a quilt, but I also think about so much more. I think of the people for whom I am making the quilt and the occasion for which I am making it. I wonder and anticipate how the quilt will be used. Will it be used and enjoyed daily, or will it be put in a cupboard, never to be seen except on special occasions? I also think about who will see it, use it, and enjoy it in the years to come.

I think of the things going on in my own life as I make each quilt. Sometimes I must stop working on a project to take care of something else—like family gatherings, special events, or my husband's emergency appendectomy. I can look at a quilt, years after I have made it, and tell you the events that were going on in my life at that time.

I think about the fabrics as I sew them into each project. So many of them bring to mind special occasions and individuals—the fabric I bought the day Luke got his driver's permit, or when I went out to lunch with my sister Heidi. Then there was the fabric that I just had to have, and then spent weeks trying to figure out the perfect quilt in which to put it. There was also the magical fabric that, the moment I found it, made everything else in the quilt fall into place.

I think about the quilts that capture special moments and memories—books I've read, childhood memories, and people or events of which I am reminded. Quilts such as "The Raspberry Thief" on page 74, are a reminder of my own childhood. I am unable to separate my feelings from the physical act of quilting. For me, the quilts that I make are truly from the heart.

The heartfelt connection begins when we first see a pattern. How we feel about it is what makes one quilt pattern say "Make me!" and another one get passed over. Those feelings continue throughout the process and are the qualities that make one person's quilt different from another's. The emotional connections, the occasions, the recipients, the colors, and the fabrics are unique to each quilter.

In this book I hope that you will find a quilt, or quilts, with which you feel a bond. Embrace those feelings and make each quilt your own.

Quiltmaking Basics

Read through this section to find all the information you'll need to get started, from choosing fabrics and rotary cutting to special piecing techniques that are used in making several of the quilts. It also covers the details of adding borders, quilting, binding, and adding a label.

Fabric Selection

The fabric you select for your quilt is its single most distinguishing feature. It will dictate the way the quilt feels, how it looks, and how long it lasts. Buy high-quality fabric, and you will have a beautiful quilt that feels wonderful now and lasts into the future. It will stand up to use, washing, and lots of loving!

When choosing fabric at a quilt store, don't be afraid to ask for help. The staff at most quilt shops are quilters, and they know their inventory! If you are having difficulty finding the fabric you want, ask. Listen to what they have to say, but don't buy any fabric unless it's what you want.

Different quilt stores carry different fabrics. If you can't find exactly what you want at one store, try another. Don't be afraid to bring fabric purchased at one store into another store to match it. The sales staff doesn't mind. If matching a fabric you already have allows them to sell you more, they still make the sale.

When I was making "Tranquility," on page 91, I had a bag of Asian-themed fabric that I hauled into any quilt store I could find. By bringing it with me I was able to avoid duplications and add the right colors. It also allowed clerks to see exactly what I was looking for, and many showed me fabrics that I would not have considered or even known about otherwise.

If you don't have the luxury of several local quilt stores, don't be afraid to buy fabric online. There are several excellent quilt stores that sell fabric online. Initially I will only order one or two fabrics so that I can determine the quality of the fabric, the shipping and handling costs, as well as the time that it takes to receive it. I bookmark the stores that I like on my computer and keep a list of those that I don't.

Online quilt stores are also an excellent source of 108"-wide backing fabric. You would be amazed at the selection of wide backing fabrics that are now available in a broad array of styles and colors. There are several reasons why I like to use wide backings:

- It's usually cheaper than buying 44" yardage when making a large quilt.
- I prefer not to piece together 2- or 3-yard lengths of fabric for a quilt back.
- I like the sense of visual continuity in a backing made from a single piece of wide yardage.

Rotary Cutting

All the fabric pieces in this book can be cut with a rotary cutter and include a ¼" seam allowance in the measurements.

1. To cut strips, fold the fabric in half, selvage to selvage, aligning the grain lines and placing the folded edge closest to you on your cutting mat.
2. Use your rotary cutter and long ruler to trim the left edge from your fabric. To ensure a straight cut that is perpendicular to the fold, align a square ruler with the folded edge of the fabric and place the long ruler against the left side. Remove the square ruler and cut along the right edge of the long ruler.

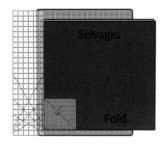

3. To cut the strips, align the appropriate measurement of your ruler with the left edge of your fabric. For example, to cut a 2½"-wide strip, place the 2½" line on the edge of the fabric.

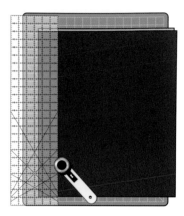

4. To cut individual squares, cut a strip the required width and trim up the selvage edge. Then, align the appropriate measurement of your ruler with the left edge of the fabric and cut.

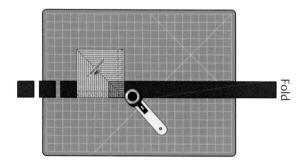

5. For individual rectangles, cut the strips as wide as the smaller dimension of the rectangle and then cut the larger dimension of the rectangle from the strips. For example, if you need 2½" x 9½" rectangles, cut the fabric strips 2½" wide and then cut the strips into 9½" pieces.

Fussy Cutting

Fussy cutting is a wonderful way to personalize your quilts. It allows you to make use of fun or interesting fabrics by centering a specific design in a cut square. Fussy-cut motifs can be used as the focal point of a quilt, such as in "Karin's Fancy" (page 51), as well as for hidden surprises, such as in "Flotsam and Jetsam" (page 40) and "Make Way for Ducklings" (page 60).

Fussy cutting requires more fabric than is needed for straight cutting fabric strips. If you're fussy cutting a few squares out of a variety of fabrics as in "Flotsam and Jetsam," this won't significantly increase the amount of fabric required to make your quilt. If, however, you're planning on cutting all your fussy-cut blocks from a single fabric, you'll have to purchase more yardage. The pattern and design of the fabric that you select will affect how much more you'll need. Refer to "Determining Yardage for Fussy Cutting" on page 9 for additional details. To fussy cut a specific design from fabric, follow the steps below.

1. Make sure that the printed motif is the appropriate size for the finished square in the desired block. The block in "Make Way for Ducklings" requires 2½" x 2½" squares that will finish at 2" square. That means the motif must fit inside the 2" square. In the fabric shown below, the duck motif measures 1¾" x 1¼", so it will work for the 2" square space.

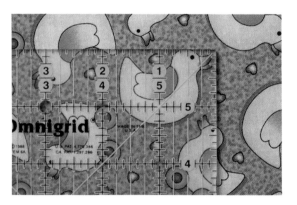

2. Determine the center point of the square and center the fabric motif under your ruler. To find the center point, divide the cut dimension in half. For example, the center point of a 2½" square is 1¼", so center the motif under the 1¼" intersection on the ruler.

3. Cut along the edges of the ruler on the top and right sides.

4. Lift the ruler and rotate the fabric 180°. Align the ruler so that the two cut edges are at the 2½" line. Cut the two remaining sides. The design should be centered within the square.

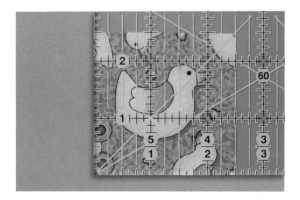

Determining Yardage for Fussy Cutting

To determine how much fabric to purchase, spread the fabric out to see how many squares you can get out of a specific quantity of fabric without overlapping. Divide the number of squares needed by the number you can get from that quantity of fabric; use the answer to multiply the original quantity of fabric. For example, let's say you can fussy cut 10 squares from of ¼ yard of the fabric you selected. The project calls for 30 squares. Divide 30 by 10 and you get 3. You would need three ¼-yard pieces, or ¾ yard total, to ensure that you have enough fabric to cut 30 squares.

For fussy cutting, it's not unusual to have to buy double or more the amount of fabric than you'd buy if you were cutting the fabric in strips. I always round up when I know I'm going to fussy cut a project. The nice thing is that if I end up with extra fabric, I can always include it in another quilt.

Sewing

All the blocks in this book are sewn using a ¼" seam allowance with fabric pieced right sides together. When I'm done sewing, I feed a small scrap of fabric under the needle and sew part way through it. The scrap fabric keeps the threads from getting tangled when I begin to sew again. When I'm sewing a number of similar units, I chain stitch them as follows.

1. Match the fabric pieces you're going to sew with right sides together.
2. Start stitching on a fabric scrap, stopping just before the end of the scrap. Without cutting the thread, place the first fabric pair in front of the presser foot, and then sew using a ¼" seam allowance; do not remove the pair from the machine.

3. Align the next pair in front of the presser foot. After sewing the first pair, sew the next pair, leaving a few stitches between them. Repeat until you've sewn all the pairs together.

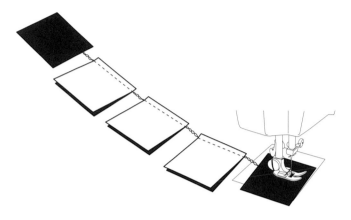

4. Feed a scrap of fabric under the needle and stitch onto it. Clip the sewn pairs from the scrap fabric, and then cut the pairs apart.

Pressing and Pinning

Taking the time to press and pin increases the overall accuracy of your piecing and makes block and quilt construction much easier. It allows pieced fabrics to lie flatter and look neater. When beginning to sew a quilt block, plan ahead to determine where seams will come together and press pieces so seams will align. This will make the process of pinning much easier.

For the projects in this book, I've included pressing directions to assist with construction of the blocks. The side that you will be pressing toward should be facing up when pressing.

When sewing together two pieced units, take care to align seams that are supposed to meet. Matching seams keeps the visual line of the block unbroken. Locking seams allowances together is the easiest way to match seams, not only with squares and rectangles, but with half-square-triangle units as well. Pressing the seam allowances in opposite directions when units are to be joined allows the bulk of the seam allowances to butt together, forming a tight, perfectly aligned seam.

Aligning the top raw edges of the two units to be pieced, begin to slide the top edges of the units against each other horizontally until the seam allowances bump into each other. The seams are now aligned and "locked" or butted together. Pin through the center of the seam to keep them aligned.

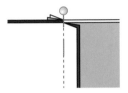

Pinning a locked seam

If you have blocks with seams that don't line up exactly, pinning can help correct the problem. Pin at all the points where the seams should match. This will help you determine where the blocks are uneven. Pin the center where there is excess fabric to the center of the corresponding piece. If the space is longer than a couple of inches, or if there is a large discrepancy between the blocks, pin again as necessary. When you sew the pieces together, leave the pins in place until they are almost under the needle. This forces the sewing machine to sew the excess fabric rather than pushing it toward the next pin. My personal rule of thumb is, "When in doubt, pin."

Special Piecing Methods

Rather than cutting and sewing triangles, I prefer to use methods that require simply cutting squares, marking them, and then sewing on the line. I use a .05 mm mechanical pencil for marking the fabric. It stays sharp and leaves a nice, crisp line.

The directions for half-square-triangle units, quarter-square-triangle units, Mary's Triangles blocks, and flying-geese units call for drawing parallel lines, and then sewing on the lines to make more than one unit at a time. I find that this method increases my accuracy in piecing and I don't have to remember to put a ¼" presser foot on the machine.

Half-Square-Triangle Units

There are many ways to make half-square-triangle units. I prefer the following method of construction for its accuracy, particularly for scrap quilts where I want to include the maximum variety of fabrics. This technique requires a 6" Bias Square® ruler.

1. Gather the fabric squares as indicated in the quilt pattern. They have been cut oversized so that you can trim the units to be perfectly accurate later. Set aside the darker of the two fabrics.

2. With the wrong side of the lighter fabric square face up, align the ¼" line of a ruler with the diagonal corners of the square. Draw a diagonal line. Rotate the square 180º and repeat, drawing a second line ¼" from the center, parallel to the first.

Two drawn lines, each
¼" from the center

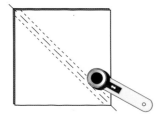

One-Line Option

Note that you can draw a single line diagonally through the center of the square, and then sew parallel lines ¼" on either side of the line. Use a ¼" presser foot after drawing a single line.

3. Layer the marked square with a darker square, right sides together. With the drawn lines on top, sew the squares together by chain sewing, first on one of the drawn lines, and then on the other. Cut the sewn squares in half diagonally between the sewn lines. Press as specified in the pattern directions, usually toward the darker fabric.

4. The half-square-triangle units will be oversized. Trim to size by aligning the diagonal line on the Bias Square ruler with the seam line of the block. The edge of the ruler should be close to the edge of the block. Trim the right side and top of the block. Rotate the block 180º and align the trimmed edges of the square with the lines on the ruler that represent the unfinished size of the square as specified in the project instructions. Trim the excess fabric from the remaining side and top edges.

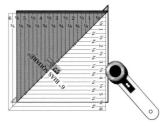

Quarter-Square-Triangle Units

Quarter-square-triangle units are made in the same basic manner as half-square-triangle units, with just a few additional steps. You will need two half-square-triangle units to make two quarter-square-triangle units.

1. Follow steps 1–3 for half-square-triangle units. Do not trim.

2. On the wrong side of one half-square-triangle unit, draw parallel diagonal lines ¼" on either side of the center, bisecting the sewn seam.

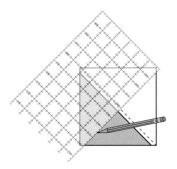

3. Layer the marked unit with an unmarked unit, right sides together and center seams aligned. The colors directly on top of each other will be next to each other in the completed quarter-square-triangle unit. Sew on the drawn lines, and then cut the squares in half diagonally between the sewn lines. Press the seam allowances to one side.

4. The quarter-square-triangle units will be oversized. Place the diagonal line of the Bias Square on one of the seam lines. Align the other seam with the lines on the ruler that represent the unfinished size of the quarter-square-triangle unit, as specified in the project instructions. Trim the right side and top of the square.

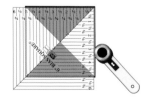

5. Rotate the block 180° and align the diagonal line and the seam line. Align the trimmed edges of the square with the lines on the ruler that represent the unfinished size of the square (5"). Trim the excess fabric from the remaining side and top. You will now have a perfect square and accurate quarter-square-triangle unit.

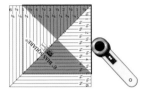

Mary's Triangles Blocks

I first learned how to make Mary's Triangles blocks when I bought Sally Schneider's book *Scrapmania: More Quick-Pieced Scrap Quilts* (Martingale & Company, 1994) several years ago. Sally had developed an easy way to make these pieced-square units and named them after her friend Mary. In the intervening years I have not found any method that works nearly as well.

For each pair of Mary's Triangles blocks, you will need two squares, two rectangles, and one larger rectangle. The project instructions will tell you the sizes to cut.

1. Sew the squares and small rectangles together in pairs. Press the seam allowances toward the squares. Sew these units together, along their long sides, so that the squares are at opposite ends.

2. Clip the seam allowance between the two squares and press the seam allowance of each section toward the rectangle.

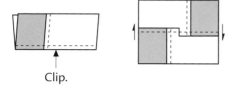

Clip.

3. On the wrong side of the pieced-rectangle unit, draw a 45° diagonal line beginning at the corner; it should just touch the tip of the square in the middle of the unit and then continue to the opposite edge. Repeat, drawing another diagonal line parallel to the first, which just touches the tip of the other square and ends at the opposite corner in the pieced-rectangle unit. This can be done easily by aligning the center diagonal line of the Bias Square, or 6" x 6" ruler and the short edge of the rectangle, and then drawing along the side.

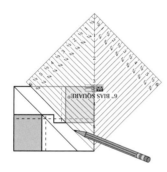

4. Layer the pieced rectangle with the large rectangle, right sides together. Sew on the drawn lines; then cut the units apart between the sewn lines. Press the seam allowances toward the large triangle.

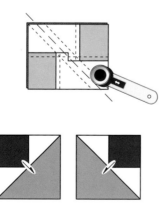

Flying Geese

Another easy method of construction that I found in someone else's quilt book, in this case Evelyn Sloppy's *40 Fabulous Quick-Cut Quilts* (Martingale & Company, 2005), is for flying geese. It's an amazing technique that allows you to make flying-geese units without cutting and sewing a single triangle! One large square and four small squares will make four flying-geese units.

1. Gather the fabric pieces as specified in the quilt pattern.
2. On the wrong side of all the small squares, draw two parallel diagonal lines ¼" from either side of the center.

Bigger Is Not Better

Carefully cut the small squares to the exact size given in the pattern. Anything larger can result in excess fabric showing at the apex of the flying-geese units.

3. Align two small squares diagonally on top of a large square, right sides together. The corners of the small squares will overlap. Sew on the drawn lines and cut the sections apart. Press the seam allowances toward the small triangles.

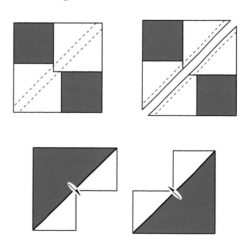

4. Align one of the remaining small squares with one of the large units so the drawn line goes from the corner of the triangle to the space between the small triangles. Sew on the drawn lines; cut apart between the sewn lines. Press the seam allowance toward the small triangle.

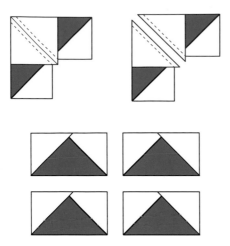

5. Trim the completed flying-geese unit to the size indicated in the quilt pattern. Be sure to leave a ¼" seam allowance beyond the tip of the triangle.

Borders

For best results, always measure your quilt before cutting border strips. Because the edges of the quilt can stretch during construction, measure the length and width of the quilt through the center to determine the correct length for the border strips. The borders for the quilts in this book are cut along the crosswise grain of the fabric and sewn together to achieve the needed length.

Borders with Butted Corners

1. Measure the length of the quilt through the center and cut side border strips to the determined length, piecing as necessary. Mark the center of the quilt at the sides and the center of the border strips. Pin the border strips to the sides of the quilt, aligning ends and center marks. Using a ¼" seam allowance, stitch along the long edges, and then press the seam allowances toward the borders.

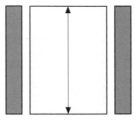

Measure the length through the center.

2. Measure the width of the quilt through the center, including the side borders just added, and cut top and bottom border strips to the determined length, piecing as necessary Mark the center of the quilt edge and the center of the border strips. Pin the border strips to the top and bottom of the quilt, aligning ends and center marks. Using a ¼" seam allowance, stitch along the long edges and then press the seam allowances toward the borders.

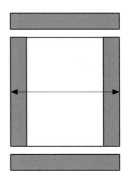

Measure the width through the center.

Borders with Corner Squares

1. Measure the width and length of the quilt through the center and then cut border strips to the determined lengths. Piece border strips as necessary to get the needed lengths.

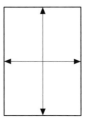

2. Mark the center of the quilt edges on all sides and the centers of the border strips. Pin the side border strips to the sides of the quilt, aligning ends and center marks. Using a ¼" seam allowance, stitch along the long edges, and then press the seam allowances toward the borders.

3. Sew corner squares or pieced corner units (equal to the cut width of the border strips) to each end of the top and bottom border strips. Press the seam allowances toward the border strips. Pin the border strips to the top and bottom of the quilt, matching seams. Using a ¼" seam allowance, stitch along the long edges, and then press the seam allowances toward the borders.

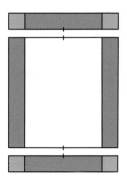

Borders with Mitered Corners

1. Measure the length and width of the quilt through the center, add two times the width of the borders, and then add 4" to 5". Cut the border strips to the determined lengths, piecing as necessary to achieve the needed length.

2. Mark the center of the quilt edges on all sides and mark the center of each border.

3. Match the centers of the quilt and borders and sew the side borders to the quilt, beginning and ending the sewing ¼" from the corners of the quilt. The borders will be longer than the quilt. Do not trim.

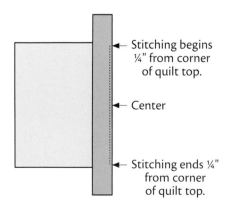

Stitching begins ¼" from corner of quilt top.

Center

Stitching ends ¼" from corner of quilt top.

4. Repeat for the top and bottom borders, again starting and stopping ¼" from the edge of the quilt.

5. Lay one corner of the quilt right side up on your sewing table or other hard surface. Lay one border strip out flat and fold its corresponding border strip up and under at a 45° angle, so that it overlaps the first one with right sides together. Press a crease in the folded edge and pin in place.

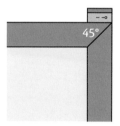

45°

6. Fold the quilt right sides together so that the long border sides overlap. This will unfold the creased border. Beginning at the inside edge of the quilt, sew on the creased line to the edge of the border.

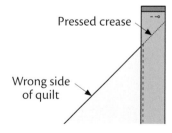

Pressed crease

Wrong side of quilt

7. Unfold the quilt and check the right side of the quilt to make sure there are no puckers and that the seam lies flat. Trim the excess fabric, leaving a ¼" seam allowance, and press the seam allowance open. Repeat for the remaining corners.

Assembling the Quilt Sandwich

When the quilt top is complete, the next step is to get it ready for quilting by layering the backing, batting, and quilt top to create the quilt sandwich. Begin by pressing both the quilt top and the backing fabric. You want them to be as wrinkle free as possible.

1. When both the top and backing are pressed, lay the backing fabric down on your work surface so that the wrong side of the backing is facing up. Masking tape or woodworking clamps work well to keep the backing fabric pulled taut. Do not stretch the fabric.

2. Center the batting over the backing fabric. Use your hands to press any wrinkles out of the batting. Work from the center out toward the edges so that excess batting gets pushed beyond your backing.

3. When the batting is flat and free of wrinkles, center the quilt, right side up, over the backing and batting. Starting at the center and working outward, ease any wrinkles out of the top.

4. Pin or thread baste the quilt sandwich together, working from the center outward. For machine quilting, I prefer to pin using 1" brass safety pins, pinning every 6" to 8". When pinning, I try to anticipate where I will be doing my straight-line quilting and avoid putting pins in that path. This allows me to sew continuous lines without having to stop and remove safety pins.

Quilting

It is often said that the quilting makes the quilt. The quilting is definitely another opportunity for you to personalize your quilt or connect it with the recipient. Like selecting the fabric and choosing the colors, the quilting you choose makes it uniquely yours. Don't be afraid to challenge yourself to try something new. I was scared to death to quilt big brown footballs in the middle of my beautiful scrap quilt, but I love the way "First and Goal" turned out.

Invest in an even-feed walking foot for your sewing machine and buy or make an extension table. These two items make machine quilting a much easier process. If possible, buy an even feed walking foot designed specifically for your machine. It will tend to work better than a generic foot. Extension tables can be ordered online or through your local quilt shop or sewing-machine dealer.

If you are unsure of your skills, take a class or read one of the quilt books that are available. Most quilt shops offer beginning machine-quilting classes and their staff can assist you in strengthening your skills. Books such as *Machine Quilting Made Easy!* (Martingale & Company, 1994) by Maurine Noble offer practical suggestions and tips for making your quilting striking.

Planning Your Quilting

Before I begin to quilt any project, I spend a lot of time thinking about what I want my finished quilt to look like and what elements of the top I want to accentuate or highlight. One of the best ways I have found to do this is to make a black-and-white photocopy of the quilt top, either printed from my computer or from the pattern in the book. I don't want the colors, just the design elements in the top itself. Working with a photocopy, here are my methods for deciding how to quilt.

- Create a master plan. Using a pencil, I draw where I think I might want to quilt. The contrast between the photocopied quilt and the shiny pencil marks allows me to evaluate the plans. In this manner, I come up with a master quilting plan. If I have several ideas I want to evaluate I will draw different ideas in each corner of the quilt so that I can compare the way they look. Seeing it drawn out on paper helps to clarify things for me.

- Quilt straight lines first. I always begin with whatever straight-line quilting I intend to do. Some quilts consist of just straight-line quilting and others are a mix of straight lines and free-motion quilting. There are numerous books and patterns designed specifically for machine quilting with ideas and suggestions for free-motion quilting. Designs can range from very traditional hand-quilting patterns modified for machine quilting to designs that are very modern and whimsical.

- Use your imagination. Find an element from one of your fabrics that you can modify into a quilting design. Use your children's hand- or footprints as your quilting motif. I have many quilting pattern books, but I just as frequently get my patterns from cookie cutters or from doing an image search on the Internet to look for a simple line drawing of the shape I want.

- Take advantage of technology. Use a copy machine or your computer and play with the size of the motif you choose. Just because the design is 4" square, it doesn't mean that you have to keep it that way. I will frequently print a design out four or five times in ¼" increments. I then rough cut around the shapes and lay them on top of my quilt to see which one fits the space the best.

The quilting is a wonderful opportunity to make a quilt unique. Have fun!

Choosing Quilting Thread

Don't be afraid to use a variety of threads in your quilting. I prefer to piece with silk-finish cotton and often do the quilting with it as well, but I have found that changing the weight and type of thread in the quilting adds dimension to the top. I am especially partial to Valdani and King Tut threads. They are strong, beautiful, and work wonderfully in my machine. I don't use many synthetic threads, but there are many excellent synthetic threads available. *Machine Quilting with Decorative Threads* (Martingale & Company, 1998) by Maurine Noble and Elizabeth Hendricks is a wonderful resource for the thread and needle chart that it includes.

The color of the thread is as important as the type of thread you use. The colors that you select for your quilting will directly influence the feeling of the quilt. Do you want the thread to match, highlight, or contrast with the quilt? Do you want it to draw your eye to an element or tone down and minimize attention to an area? Answer these questions and you will have a better idea of where to use different colors and where not to.

In "Puss in the Corner . . . Mice on the Run" on page 69, I wanted the quilting to be a subtle surprise, and so I chose colors that would not stand out from the background fabric at a distance. To see the mice and cat, you need to look beyond the obvious. With "She Who Dares" on page 82, I wanted to draw your eye to the purple lattice; so instead of quilting with a white thread to match the background fabric, I chose purple to provide a contrast.

Binding

Carefully trim the excess batting and backing fabric even with the edges of your quilt top. Then cut the required number of 2½"-wide binding strips for your project. Binding strips cut 2½" wide will result in a binding that finishes at about ½". For a narrower binding, cut narrower strips. Follow these steps to sew the binding strips together and onto the quilt:

1. Lay out the first binding strip right side up. Put a second binding strip, right sides together, on top of the end of the first strip at a 90° angle. Mark a diagonal line from the upper-left side to the lower-right side of the crossed binding strips and sew on the line. Trim the excess fabric to create a ¼" seam allowance. Press the seam allowance open. Repeat to add the remaining binding strips.

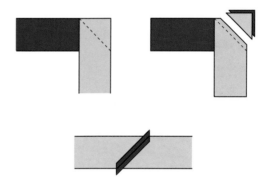

2. Fold the long binding strip in half lengthwise, wrong sides together, and press.

3. Starting at the point midway along the side or bottom edge of your quilt, align the raw edges of your binding strip with the edge of the quilt. Hold or pin the binding strip in place. Using a ¼" seam allowance, begin sewing about 10" from the end of the binding strip. Use an even-feed walking foot if you have one to help keep the layers from shifting. Stitch slowly, keeping the edges aligned. Stop sewing approximately ¼" from the corner.

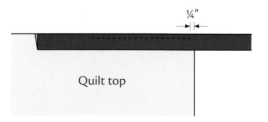

Quilt top

4. Rotate your quilt 90° so that the side of the quilt with the binding is now at the top. Move the quilt out from under the needle and fold the binding up toward the sewn edge until the fold forms a 45° angle. Hold the fold in place with one hand and fold the remainder of the binding strip back down so that the raw edges of the binding line up with the side of the quilt and the fold is even with the top edge. Using a ¼" seam allowance, begin sewing at the folded edge and continue down the side of the quilt, stopping ¼" from the next corner

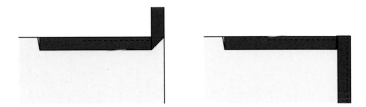

5. Repeat the mitering process at each corner. Stop stitching approximately 10" before the beginning end of the binding strip. Lay the beginning of the binding strip flat along the edge of the quilt top, and then overlap the end of the binding strip on top of it. Trim the binding strip so that the overlap is 2½" (or the width of your cut binding).

6. Unfold both ends of the binding strip and then align them, right sides together, at a right angle, just as you did when making the binding strips (see step 1). Draw a diagonal line as shown and pin in place.

Pin ends together.
Draw diagonal line.

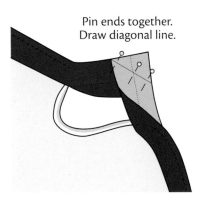

7. Sew on the drawn line. Before trimming the fabric, check to see that the binding strip fits correctly along the quilt top. Trim, leaving a ¼" seam allowance, and refold the binding strip in half wrong sides together. Align the binding with the edge of the quilt and sew into place.

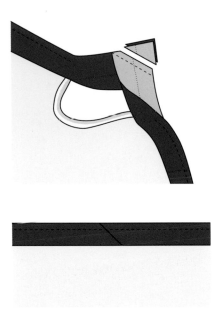

8. Working from the back of the quilt, fold the binding over the edge and pin into place. Using a thread that blends with the binding fabric, blindstitch the binding to the back of the quilt. At the corners, the binding should form a smooth 45° angle on the front and back of the quilt. Sew the miters into place at each corner.

Quilt back

Labels

I make labels for all of my quilts. This is an important part of your quilt, so don't forget to include it. I include the name of the quilt, the date I completed it, and my name and hometown. If it was made for a specific occasion, I note that on the label as well.

I've found that high-quality, solid-colored cotton in a light color works best for labels. Fabric with a pattern does not absorb the ink evenly. I stabilize the label fabric first by ironing freezer paper onto the back. I then use Pigma permanent fabric pens to draw and color the designs. The freezer paper keeps the fabric from moving while I am writing or drawing. I draw guidelines on the dull side of the freezer paper to ensure that my writing is straight and to block out any areas for designs. Remove the freezer paper before attaching the label to your quilt.

Have fun with your quilt labels. Let them be an extension of yourself or of your quilt. You don't have to be artistic to make creative and fun labels. Permanent fabric ink can be stamped with a rubber stamp and colored in with fabric pens. Draw out an idea on paper to practice, and then trace over it when you have it just the way you want it. Embellish a simple label with buttons or beads to give it some sparkle.

To make the label for "Karin's Fancy" on page 51, I used one of the penguin designs from the fabric in the quilt top. I took an extra square, taped it onto a window, and traced over it using a fabric pen. I then turned it into a snow globe by cutting a circle shape and placing it on a pedestal. I added white seed beads to create the shaken snow. It was a simple idea that added a great deal of whimsy to the quilt.

Cotton Candy

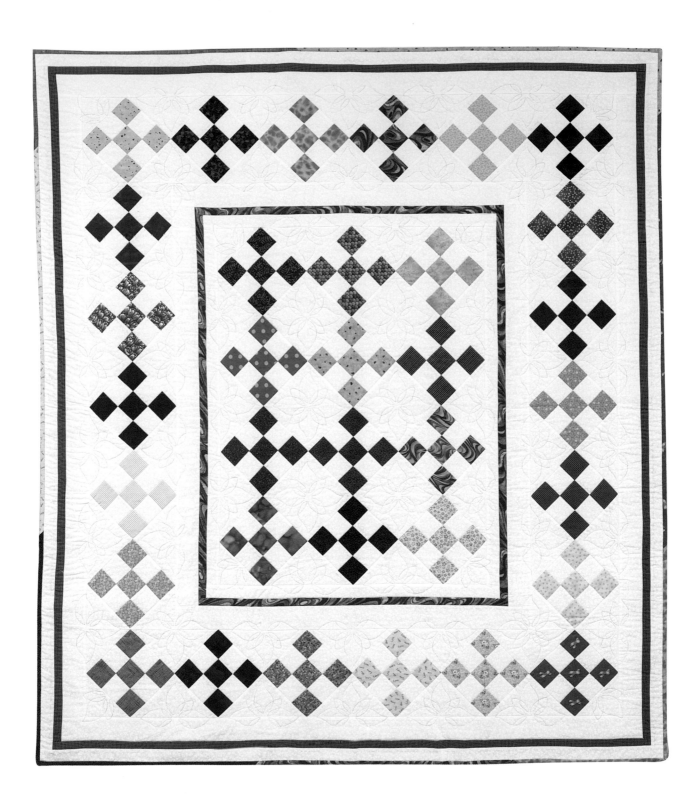

I love the fact that this is probably the easiest quilt in this book, using the simple Nine Patch block, but because of the quilting it has quite a sophisticated feel. I wanted to play with quilting designs by using a complete design, and then breaking it into sections without making the design itself smaller. This quilt is easy to piece and easy to experiment with—use your favorite colors for the blocks, or make it totally scrappy to use up your leftover fabrics.

Finished Quilt Size: 59½" x 68"
Finished Block Size: 6" x 6" (34 total)

Materials

Yardages are based on 42"-wide fabric unless otherwise noted.

3¾ yards of white fabric for blocks and borders

1½ yards *total* of assorted pink fabrics for the blocks, border blocks, and binding

⅓ yard of pink fabric B for narrow outer border

¼ yard of pink fabric A for narrow inner border

3¾ yards *or* 1⅞ yards of 108"-wide fabric for the backing

64" x 73" piece of batting

Cutting

All measurements include ¼"-wide seam allowances.

From the assorted pink fabrics, cut:

170 squares, 2½" x 2½"

7 strips, 2½" x 42" (or enough 2½"-wide strips to total 270")

From the white fabric, cut:

9 strips, 2½" x 42"; cut into 136 squares, 2½" x 2½"

1 strip, 6½" x 42"; cut into 6 squares, 6½" x 6½"

3 strips, 10" x 42"; cut into 12 squares, 10" x 10"; cut the squares twice diagonally to make 48 quarter-square triangles (2 are extra)

2 strips, 5½" x 42"; cut into 10 squares, 5½" x 5½"; cut the squares once diagonally to make 20 half-square triangles

10 strips, 1¾" x 42"

10 strips, 2¾" x 42"

From pink fabric A, cut:

3 strips, 1¼" x 42"

From pink fabric B, cut:

7 strips, 1¼" x 42"

Assembling the Blocks

1. Sew pink 2½" squares to opposite sides of 68 white 2½" squares. Press the seam allowances toward the pink squares.

2. Sew white 2½" squares to opposite sides of 34 pink 2½" squares. Press the seam allowances toward the pink squares.

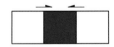

3. Sew the units from step 1 to both long sides of the units from step 2. Press the seam allowances toward the pink sections. Make 34 blocks.

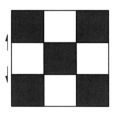

Make 34.

Assembling and Finishing

1. Use 12 of the completed blocks for the center of the quilt. Sew white 6½" squares to one side of six of the completed blocks. Press the seam allowances toward the white squares.

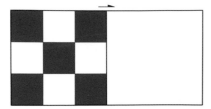

Make 6.

2. Arrange the 12 blocks, 10 large white triangles, and four small white triangles as shown. Align the right angles of the side triangles with the blocks and center the blocks on the long edge of the corner triangles. The triangles are cut slightly oversized so that you can straighten the edges later. Sew the blocks into diagonal rows; press toward the white fabric. Join the rows to complete the center section; press the seam allowances in one direction.

3. Trim the edge of the center section, leaving a ¼" seam allowance beyond the pink tips on the blocks.

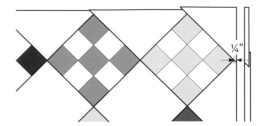

4. Referring to "Borders with Butted Corners" on page 14, measure, cut, and sew the 1¾" white inner-border strips to the sides of the quilt, and then to the top and bottom. Repeat for the 1¼" pink fabric A border strips and 2¾" white border strips. Press the seam allowances outward.

5. Using the remaining small white triangles, center and sew the wide side of two triangles onto adjoining corners of eight Nine Patch blocks. Press the seam allowances toward the white fabric.

Make 8.

6. Using eight large white triangles, sew the short side of one triangle onto the upper-right side of the units from step 5 as shown to make eight border end sections. Press the seam allowances toward the white triangles.

Make 8.

7. Sew the short side of the remaining large white tri-angles onto opposite sides of the 14 remaining Nine Patch blocks as shown. Press the seam allowances toward the white triangles.

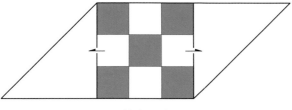

Make 14.

8. Sew three completed border sections together to make one side border. Match the seams so that the Nine Patch blocks align tip to tip; press. Make two.

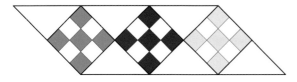

Make 2.

Detail of quilting motif variations in blocks and borders

9. Sew a border end section from step 6 to each end of the border strips to complete the side borders. There should be five blocks in each border strip. Carefully trim the sides, leaving a ¼" seam allowance beyond the pink points. Sew the borders to the sides of the quilt; press.

10. Repeat the process for the top and bottom borders, using six blocks in each border. Pin the top and bottom borders to the quilt, carefully aligning the points of the end blocks with the points on the pieced side borders. Sew and press.

11. Measure, cut, and sew the white 2¾" inner-border strips to the sides of the quilt first, and then to the top and bottom. Repeat for the pink fabric B 1¼" border strips and white 1¾" border strips. Press seam allowances outward.

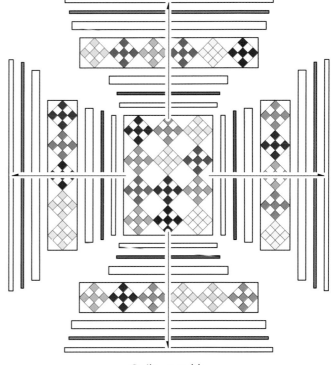

Quilt assembly

12. Assemble the quilt sandwich and quilt as desired. Bind the edges using the pink 2½" strips; add a label. Refer to the finishing techniques beginning on page 16 in "Quiltmaking Basics" for further details as needed.

The Cougarine

24

My sister-in-law Cheryl really likes navy blue and burgundy together, so I made this quilt to try out the color combination using the One Union Square block. When my family saw it, they decided it looked like what you would get if you crossed the Washington State University colors of crimson and gray (my alma mater) with maize and blue, the colors of my husband's alma mater, the University of Michigan. Since the WSU mascot is the cougar and Michigan's is the wolverine, this quilt immediately became "The Cougarine." Have fun making the quilt as shown, or substitute your favorite color combination or your own school colors.

Finished Quilt Size: 59½" x 70"
Finished Block Size: 9" x 9" (30 total)

Materials

Yardages are based on 42"-wide fabric unless otherwise noted.

3 yards of burgundy fabric for blocks and border

2⅞ yards of cream fabric for blocks and sashing

1½ yards of dark blue fabric for blocks, sashing star points, and binding

1⅛ yards of light blue fabric for blocks, sashing squares, and border

3¾ yards *or* 1¾ yards of 108"-wide fabric for backing

64" x 74" piece of batting

6" Bias Square ruler

Cutting

All measurements include ¼"-wide seam allowances.

From the cream fabric, cut:

10 strips, 3" x 42"; cut into 120 squares, 3" x 3"

6 strips, 2" x 42"; cut into 120 squares, 2" x 2"

4 strips, 4¾" x 42"; cut into 30 squares, 4¾" x 4¾"

13 strips, 2" x 42"; cut into 49 strips, 2" x 9½"

From the burgundy fabric, cut:

10 strips, 3" x 42"; cut into 120 squares, 3" x 3"

8 strips, 4¾" x 42"; cut into 60 squares, 4¾" x 4¾"

7 strips, 3½" x 42"

From the light blue fabric, cut:

7 strips, 2" x 42"; cut into 140 squares, 2" x 2"

3 strips, 3½" x 42"; cut into 30 squares, 3½" x 3½"

7 strips, 1½" x 42"

From the dark blue fabric, cut:

4 strips, 4¾" x 42"; cut into 30 squares, 4¾" x 4¾"

4 strips, 2" x 42"; cut into 80 squares, 2" x 2"

7 strips, 2½" x 42"

Assembling the Blocks

1. Referring to "Half-Square-Triangle Units" on page 10, use the cream and the burgundy 3" squares to make 240 half-square-triangle units. Trim the squares to 2".

Make 240.

2. Sew 120 half-square-triangle units to the cream 2" squares as shown. Press the seam allowances toward the cream square.

Make 120.

3. Sew the remaining half-square-triangle units to 120 light blue 2" squares. Press the seam allowances toward the light blue squares.

Make 120.

4. Sew the units from steps 2 and 3 together as shown to make 120 block corner sections; press.

Make 120.

5. Using 30 of the burgundy 4¾" squares and the dark blue 4¾" squares, assemble 120 half-square-triangle units. Press the seam allowances toward the burgundy fabric. Do not trim.

6. Use the remaining burgundy 4¾" squares and the cream 4¾" squares to assemble 120 half-square-triangle units. Press the seam allowances toward the burgundy fabric. Do not trim.

7. Referring to "Quarter-Square-Triangle Units" on page 11, pair a burgundy/dark blue half-square-triangle unit with a burgundy/cream half-square-triangle unit to assemble quarter-square-triangle units. The burgundy triangles should not be on top of each other. Press the seam allowances toward the burgundy/blue units. Trim to 3½". Make 120.

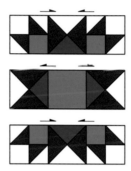

Make 120.

8. Arrange the corner sections, quarter-square-triangle units, and light blue 3½" squares into rows as shown. Sew the units into rows, pressing in the direction indicated by the arrows; then sew the rows together to form the block. Make 30 blocks.

Make 30.

Assembling and Finishing

1. Draw a diagonal line from corner to corner on the wrong side of the 80 dark blue 2" squares. Layer a square on one end of each of 49 of the cream 2" x 9½" sashing strips and sew on the drawn line. Trim off the excess fabric, leaving a ¼" seam allowance, and press the seam allowances toward the dark blue triangle.

Make 49.

2. Sew the remaining dark blue squares to the opposite end of 31 of the sashing strips. The second seam should be parallel to the first one. Trim the excess fabric and press the seam allowances toward the dark blue triangle.

Make 31.

3. Sew sashing strips with two blue corners to the side of 16 blocks. Sew sashing strips with only one blue corner to the side of 13 blocks as shown. Press toward the sashing strip.

Make 16.

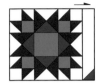

Make 9.

Make 4.

4. Sew light blue 2" squares to the blue triangle end of the 20 remaining sashing strips. Press the seam allowances toward the sashing strips.

5. Sew the five sashing strips with one blue corner to the bottom edge of the blocks as indicated.

Make 4.

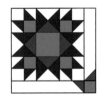

Make 1.

6. Sew the 15 remaining sashing strips with two blue corners to the bottom edge of the blocks as indicated.

Make 12.

Make 3.

7. Arrange the blocks as shown. Sew the blocks into rows, and then sew the rows together.

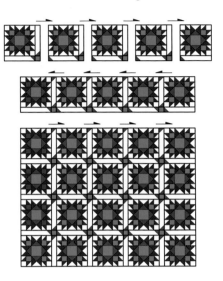

8. Referring to "Borders with Butted Corners" on page 14, measure, cut, and sew the light blue 1½" inner-border strips to the sides of the quilt, and then to the top and bottom. Repeat for the burgundy 3½" outer-border strips.

Quilt assembly

9. Assemble the quilt sandwich and quilt as desired. Bind the edges using the dark blue 2½" strips; add a label. Refer to the finishing techniques beginning on page 16 in "Quiltmaking Basics" for further details as needed.

Fanny's Dream

As I was designing this quilt on the computer, I discovered that one of the names for the block is Fanny's Favorite. I knew it was fate—one of my favorite children's books is *Fanny's Dream* by Caralyn and Mark Buehner. It's a Cinderella story, but the fairy god-mother never shows up. Instead of Prince Charming, Fanny marries Hubert and lives happily ever after anyway! I wanted the quilt to have a fairy-tale feeling, so I used soft lavenders and blues with a cream background. Make it in whatever colors make you happy.

Finished Quilt Size: 68½" x 84½"
Finished Block Size: 16" x 16" (12 total)

Materials

Yardages are based on 42"-wide fabric unless otherwise noted.

4½ yards *total* of assorted blue and lavender fabrics for blocks, pieced border, and binding

3⅞ yards of cream fabric for blocks and borders

⅜ yard of blue fabric for narrow border

5 yards *or* 2 yards of 108"-wide fabric for backing

73" x 89" piece of batting

Cutting

All measurements include ¼"-wide seam allowances.

From the cream fabric, cut:

16 strips, 2½" x 42"; cut into 232 squares, 2½" x 2½"

6 strips, 4½" x 42"; cut into:
  24 rectangles, 4½" x 5½"
  12 squares, 4½" x 4½"

2 strips, 5½" x 42"; cut into 12 squares, 5½" x 5½"

14 strips, 2" x 42"

8 strips, 2½" x 42"

From the assorted blue and lavender fabrics, cut:

48 rectangles, 2½" x 3½"

96 rectangles 2½" x 4½"

48 squares, 3" x 3"

116 squares, 4½" x 4½"

8 strips, 2½" x 42"

From the blue fabric, cut:

7 strips, 1½" x 42"

Assembling the Blocks

1. Referring to "Mary's Triangles Blocks" on page 12 and using 48 of the cream 2½" squares, the blue and lavender 2½" x 3½" rectangles, and the cream 4½" x 5½" rectangles, assemble 48 Mary's Triangles blocks. The blocks should measure 4½".

Make 48.

2. Sew a blue or lavender 2½" x 4½" rectangle to a cream side of the Mary's Triangles blocks. Press the seam allowances toward the rectangles.

3. Sew a cream 2½" square to the remaining blue and lavender 2½" x 4½" rectangles. Press the seam allowances toward the blue or lavender rectangles and sew them to the units from step 2 as shown. Press the seam allowances toward the added rectangles.

4. Referring to "Flying Geese" on page 13 and using the cream 5½" squares and blue and lavender 3" squares, make 48 flying-geese units. Trim to 2½" x 4½".

Make 48.

5. Sew the flying-geese units to 48 of the blue or lavender 4½" squares as shown. Press the seam allowances toward the squares.

6. Sew the Mary's Triangles blocks to either side of 24 of the flying-geese units, arranging them as shown. Press toward the center.

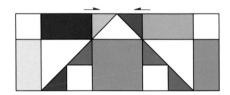

7. Sew the remaining flying-geese units from step 5 to opposite sides of the cream 4½" squares as shown. Press the seam allowances toward the blue or lavender squares.

8. Sew the units from step 6 to the top and bottom of the units from step 7 as shown. Press the seam allowances toward the center. Make 12 blocks.

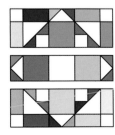
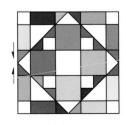

Make 12.

Assembling and Finishing

1. Arrange the blocks in four rows of three blocks each as shown. Sew the blocks into horizontal rows. Press the seam allowances in opposite directions from row to row. Join the rows together; press.

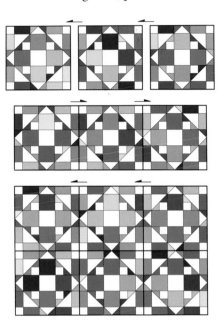

2. Referring to "Borders with Butted Corners" on page 14, measure, cut, and sew the cream 2" inner-border strips to the sides of the quilt first, and then to the top and bottom. Repeat for the light blue 1½" border strips; then add another round of cream 2" border strips.

3. Draw a diagonal line from corner to corner on the wrong side of the 136 remaining cream 2½" squares. Sew the squares to opposite corners of the remaining 68 blue and lavender 4½" squares, right sides together. Trim the excess, leaving a ¼" seam allowance. Press one corner toward the cream fabric and one toward the blue or lavender fabric.

4. Arrange the units from step 3 into two equal groups, 38 with the seam allowances pressed toward the cream in the upper-left corner and 38 with the seam allowances pressed toward the lavender or blue in the

upper-right corner. Sew these units together into pairs. Press the seam allowances to one side.

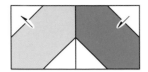

5. Sew nine units from step 4 together to form the side border. Make sure that the blue and lavender corners always adjoin to create the zigzag pattern. Make two side borders. Sew eight units from step 4 together to form the top border. Repeat to make the bottom border.

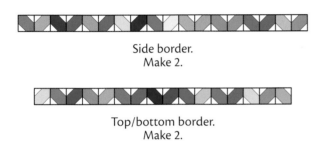

Side border.
Make 2.

Top/bottom border.
Make 2.

6. Sew the side borders to the quilt, making sure that the end blue or lavender segments point away from the quilt. Sew the top and bottom borders to the quilt so that the end blue or lavender segments point toward the quilt.

7. Sew the final cream 2½" border onto the quilt in the same manner as the other borders with butted corners.

Quilt assembly

8. Assemble the quilt sandwich and quilt as desired. Bind the edges using the blue and lavender 2½" strips; add a label. Refer to the finishing techniques beginning on page 16 in "Quiltmaking Basics" for further details as needed.

As I was experimenting with this block, Game Cocks, I became intrigued with the designs that were created when the blocks were set together. Secondary stars emerge at the block intersections. It makes a superb scrap quilt, but it would also work well with fewer fabrics for a more structured look. The elliptical shapes that form where the blocks join remind me of footballs, which inspired both the quilting design and the quilt name.

Finished Quilt Size: 69" x 84"
Finished Block Size: 15" x 15" (20 total)

Materials

Yardages are based on 42"-wide fabric unless otherwise noted.

3⅞ yards of white fabric for blocks

3¼ yards *total* of assorted colored fabrics for blocks

1 yard of blue fabric for outer border

½ yard of fuchsia fabric for inner border

⅛ yard of purple fabric for border corner squares

5 yards *or* 2⅛ yards of 108"-wide fabric for backing

¾ yard of multicolored fabric for binding

74" x 89" piece of batting

6" bias square ruler

Cutting

All measurements include ¼"-wide seam allowances.

From the white fabric, cut:

10 strips, 4½" x 42"; cut into 80 squares, 4½" x 4½"

17 strips, 2" x 42"; cut into 320 squares, 2" x 2"

12 strips, 3½" x 42"; cut into:

    80 squares, 3½" x 3½"

    80 rectangles, 2" x 3½"

From the assorted colored fabrics, cut:

80 squares, 4½" x 4½"

320 squares, 2" x 2"

80 rectangles, 2" x 3½"

20 squares, 3½" x 3½"

From the fuchsia fabric, cut:

7 strips, 2" x 42"

From the blue fabric, cut:

4 squares, 2" x 2"

8 strips, 3½" x 42"

From the purple fabric, cut:

4 squares, 3½" x 3½"

From the multicolored fabric, cut:

8 strips, 2½" x 42"

Assembling the Blocks

1. Referring to "Half-Square-Triangle Units" on page 10, make 160 half-square-triangle units using the white and the colored 4½" squares. Press the seam allowances toward the colored print. Trim the units to 3½".

Make 160.

2. Sew the colored 2" squares to the white 2" squares. Press the seam allowances toward the colored square. Sew the units together to make 160 four-patch units as shown. Press seam allowances open.

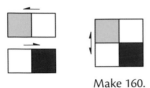

Make 160.

3. Sew the half-square-triangle units to the right side of the four-patch units as shown. Press the seam allowances toward the four-patch units.

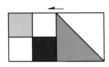

4. Sew two units from step 3 together so that the colored squares form a diagonal chain. Press the seam allowances open. Make 80.

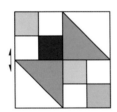

Make 80.

5. Sew the colored 2" x 3½" rectangles to the white 2" x 3½" rectangles along their long sides. Press the seam allowances toward the colored rectangles.

Make 80.

6. Sew white 3½" squares to the colored side of the rectangle pairs from step 5. Press the seam allowances toward the white squares.

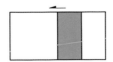

7. Sew the units from step 4 to opposite sides of 40 of the units from step 6 as shown. Press the seam allowances toward the center section.

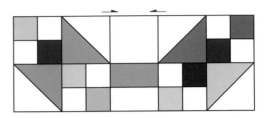

8. Sew the remaining units from step 6 to opposite sides of the colored 3½" squares as shown. Press the seam allowances toward the white rectangles.

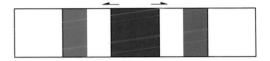

9. Sew the units from step 7 to the top and bottom of the center section from step 8. Press the seam allowances toward the center.

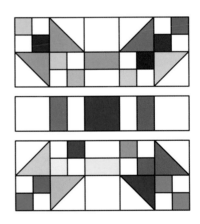

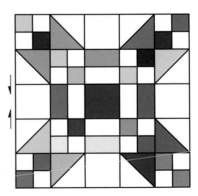

Assembling and Finishing

1. Arrange the blocks in five rows of four blocks each. Sew the blocks into horizontal rows; press the seam allowances in opposite direction from row to row. Sew the rows together; press the seam allowances in one direction.

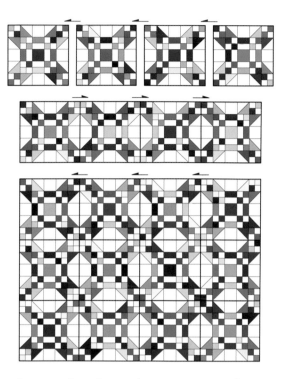

2. Referring to "Borders with Corner Squares" on page 14, measure and trim the fuchsia 2" strips to the determined length, piecing as necessary. Sew the strips to the sides of the quilt. Sew the blue 2" corner squares to each end of the top and bottom border strips, and then sew the border strips to the top and bottom of the quilt. Repeat for the blue 3½" border using the purple 3½" squares.

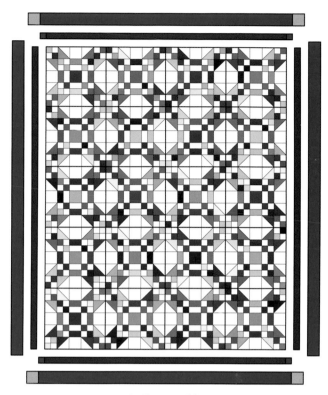

Quilt assembly

3. Assemble the quilt sandwich and quilt as desired. Use the football quilting design below in the open areas if you like. Bind the edges using the multicolored 2½" strips; add a label. Refer to the finishing techniques beginning on page 16 in "Quiltmaking Basics" for further details as needed.

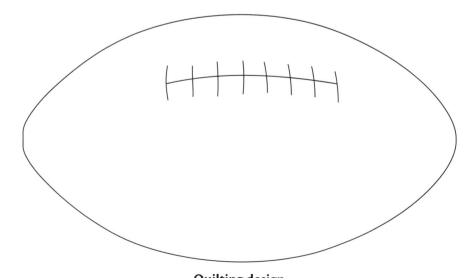

Quilting design
Enlarge pattern 125%.

Flight of Fancy

I chanced upon this setting quite by accident when using the Darting Birds block to make a thank-you quilt for a friend. I had intended to lay the blocks out in a more linear fashion, but was amazed at the wonderful woven lattice effect they created when arranged in this alternating design. To accentuate the look, I quilted diagonally along the seam lines.

If you have scraps, this is the perfect quilt. It's also ideal for including fussy-cut squares as small surprises here and there throughout the quilt.

Finished Quilt Size: 58½" x 70½"
Finished Block Size: 6" x 6" (80 total)

Materials

Yardages are based on 42"-wide fabric unless otherwise noted.

2⅞ yards of white fabric for blocks

2¾ yards of red fabric for blocks and inner and outer borders

1¾ yards *total* of assorted colored fabric for blocks

⅜ yard of light blue fabric for middle border

⅝ yard of dark blue fabric for binding

3½ yards *or* 1¾ yards of 108"-wide fabric for backing

63" x 75" piece of batting

6" Bias Square ruler

Cutting

All measurements include ¼"-wide seam allowances.

From the white fabric, cut:

22 strips, 3½" x 42"; cut into 240 squares, 3½" x 3½"

5 strips, 2½" x 42"; cut into 80 squares, 2½" x 2½"

From the red fabric, cut:

15 strips, 3½" x 42"; cut into 160 squares, 3½" x 3½"

7 strips, 2" x 42"

7 strips, 3" x 42"

From the assorted colored fabric, cut:

80 squares, 3½" x 3½"

160 squares, 2½" x 2½"

From the light blue fabric, cut:

7 strips, 1½" x 42"

From the dark blue fabric, cut:

7 strips, 2½" x 42"

Assembling the Blocks

1. Referring to "Half-Square-Triangle Units" on page 10 and using 160 white 3½" squares and the red 3½" squares, make 320 half-square-triangle units. Press the seam allowances toward the red fabric and trim the squares to 2½" x 2½". Repeat using the remaining white 3½" squares and the colored 3½" squares to make 160 units. Press the seam allowances toward the white fabric, and trim to 2½".

Make 320.   Make 160.

2. Sew 80 colored half-square-triangle units, 80 red half-square-triangle units, and the white 2½" squares together as shown. Press the seam allowances in the direction indicated by the arrows.

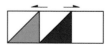

Make 80.

3. Sew a red half-square-triangle unit to each side of 80 colored 2½" squares as shown. Press the seam allowances toward the center square.

Make 80.

4. Sew a colored 2½" square, a red half-square-triangle unit, and a colored half-square-triangle unit together as shown. Press the seam allowances in the direction of the arrows. The red and colored triangles should form a V. Make 80.

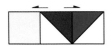

Make 80.

5. Sew the three rows made in steps 2, 3, and 4 together as shown. Press the seam allowances toward the center row.

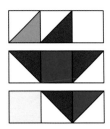 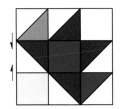

Make 80.

Assembling and Finishing

1. Sew the blocks together in groups of four. Press the seam allowances toward the colored square. The blocks will form a pinwheel. Make 20 large block units.

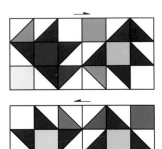 

Make 20.

2. Arrange the large blocks in five rows of four blocks each as shown. Sew the blocks into horizontal rows; press seam allowances in opposite direction from row to row. Sew the rows together; press the seam allowances in one direction.

3. Referring to "Borders with Butted Corners" on page 14, measure, cut, and sew the red 2" inner-border strips to the sides of the quilt first, and then to the top and bottom. Repeat for the light blue 1½" middle-border strips and the red 3" outer-border strips.

4. Assemble the quilt sandwich and quilt as desired. Bind the edges using the dark blue 2½" strips; add a label. Refer to the finishing techniques beginning on page 16 in "Quiltmaking Basics" for further details as needed.

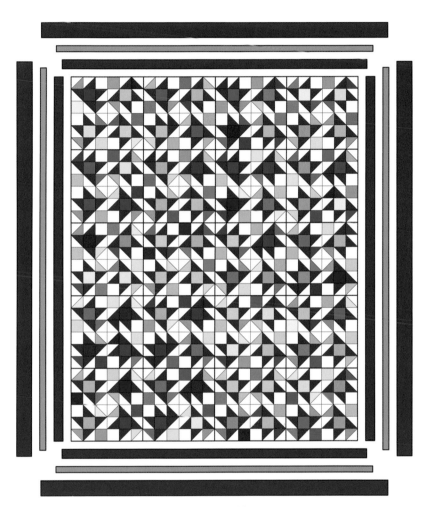

Quilt assembly

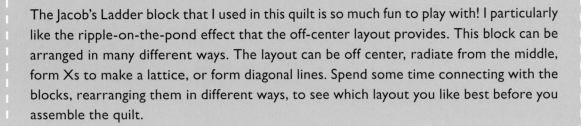

The Jacob's Ladder block that I used in this quilt is so much fun to play with! I particularly like the ripple-on-the-pond effect that the off-center layout provides. This block can be arranged in many different ways. The layout can be off center, radiate from the middle, form Xs to make a lattice, or form diagonal lines. Spend some time connecting with the blocks, rearranging them in different ways, to see which layout you like best before you assemble the quilt.

Finished Quilt Size: 62½" x 71½"
Finished Block Size: 9" x 9" (42 total)

Materials

Yardages are based on 42"-wide fabric unless otherwise noted.

3¼ yards of light blue fabric for blocks and borders

2⅜ yards of dark blue fabric for blocks and borders

1½ yards *total* of assorted colored fabrics for blocks

⅝ yard of green fabric for binding

3¾ yards or 1⅞ yards of 108"-wide fabric for backing

67" x 76" piece of batting

6" bias square ruler

Cutting

All measurements include ¼"-wide seam allowances.

From the dark blue fabric, cut:

11 strips, 4½" x 42"; cut into 84 squares, 4½" x 4½"

8 strips, 3½" x 42"

From the light blue fabric, cut:

11 strips, 4½" x 42"; cut into 84 squares, 4½" x 4½"

21 strips, 2" x 42"; cut into 420 squares, 2" x 2"

7 strips, 1½" x 42"

From the assorted colored fabrics, cut:

420 squares, 2" x 2"

From the green fabric, cut:

7 strips, 2½" x 42"

Assembling the Blocks

1. Referring to "Half-Square-Triangle Units" on page 10 and using the dark blue and the light blue 4½" squares, make 168 half-square-triangle units. Press the seam allowances toward the dark blue fabric. Trim the squares to 3½".

Make 168.

2. Sew the light blue and the colored 2" squares together in pairs; press the seam allowances toward the light blue fabric. Sew the pairs together to make 210 four-patch units as shown. Press the seam allowances to one side.

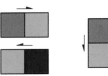

Make 210.

3. Arrange five of the four-patch units and four of the half-square-triangle units as shown. Sew the units together to make three rows and press the seam allowances in the direction indicated by the arrows. Sew the

rows together and press the seam allowances toward the top and bottom rows. Make 42 blocks.

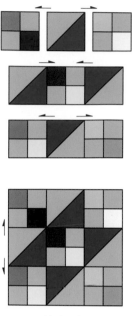

Make 42.

Assembling and Finishing

1. Arrange the blocks in seven rows of six blocks each as shown or play with the blocks to determine an alternate layout. Sew the blocks into horizontal rows, pressing the seam allowances in opposite direction from row to row. Sew the rows together; press the seam allowances in one direction.

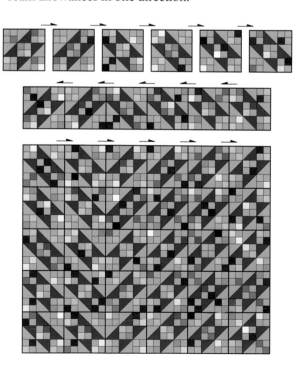

2. Referring to "Borders with Butted Corners" on page 14, measure, cut, and sew the light blue 1½" inner-border strips to the sides of the quilt, and then to the top and bottom. Repeat for the dark blue 3½" border strips.

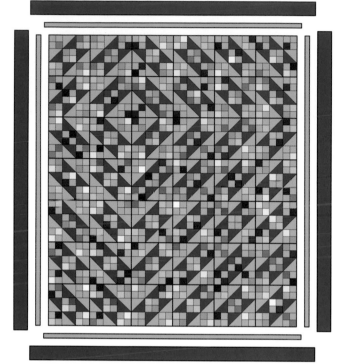

Quilt assembly

3. Assemble the quilt sandwich and quilt as desired. Bind the edges using the green 2½" strips; add a label. Refer to the finishing techniques beginning on page 16 in "Quiltmaking Basics" for further details as needed.

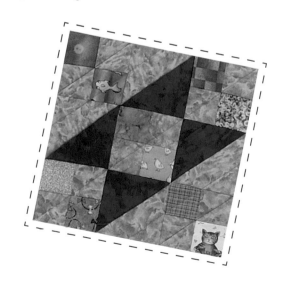

I freely admit to being a color snob. In my opinion, not all colors are created equal. Brown is a color that I usually avoid in my quilts because I think brown-toned quilts are dull and drab. (I know that's not really true.) I challenged myself to make a brown quilt that was neither of those things. I paired two different browns with pink and cream prints using the Chain and Cross block. "Hot Fudge Sundae" is the result, and I really do like it—in spite of it being brown! So, if you're like me, step out of your comfort zone and give brown a chance!

Finished Quilt Size: 68" x 83"
Finished Block Size: 13½" x 13½" (20 total)

Materials

Yardages are based on 42"-wide fabric unless otherwise noted.

3 yards of dark brown fabric for blocks and borders

1⅞ yards of cream-and-pink floral for blocks

1⅞ yards of light brown fabric for blocks and sashing

⅞ yard of dusty rose fabric for blocks, sashing squares, and binding

⅝ yard *total* of assorted pink fabrics for blocks

5 yards *or* 2 yards of 108"-wide fabric for backing

72" x 87" piece of batting

Cutting

All measurements include ¼"-wide seam allowances.

From the assorted pink fabrics, cut:

160 squares, 2" x 2"

From the cream-and-pink floral, cut:

24 strips, 2" x 42"; cut into:
    160 squares, 2" x 2"
    80 rectangles, 2" x 8"

From the light brown fabric, cut:

4 strips, 3½" x 42"; cut into 80 rectangles, 2" x 3½"

25 strips, 2" x 42"; cut into 49 rectangles, 2" x 14"

From the dusty rose fabric, cut:

3 strips, 2" x 42"; cut into 50 squares, 2" x 2"

8 strips, 2½" x 42"

From the dark brown fabric, cut:

16 strips, 2" x 42"; cut into 80 rectangles, 2" x 8"

16 strips, 3½" x 42"; cut 8 of the strips into 80 squares, 3½" x 3½"

Assembling the Blocks

1. Sew the pink 2" squares to the floral 2" squares; press the seam allowances toward the pink squares. Sew the units together in pairs to make 80 four-patch units.

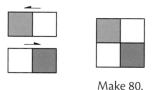

Make 80.

2. Sew the four-patch units to opposite sides of 40 of the light brown 2" x 3½" rectangles. The pink squares should form a V. Press the seam allowances toward the light brown rectangles.

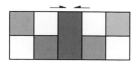

Make 40.

3. Sew the remaining light brown 2" x 3½" rectangles to 20 rose 2" squares. Press the seam allowances toward the light brown rectangles.

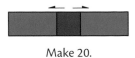

Make 20.

4. Sew the four-patch units from step 2 to the top and bottom of the units from step 3 as shown. The pink squares should form an X within the block. Press the seam allowances toward the center. Make 20 blocks.

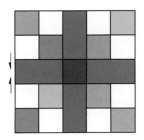

Make 20.

5. Sew the dark brown rectangles and the floral rectangles together in pairs. Sew and press carefully in order to avoid distorting the units. Press toward the brown fabric. Sew dark brown squares to opposite sides of 40 of the brown and floral units. Press the seam allowances toward the brown and floral units.

Make 80.   Make 40.

6. Sew the units from step 5 to the blocks from step 4 as shown, ensuring that the brown print is adjacent to the center section. Press the seam allowances toward the brown fabric. Make 20 blocks.

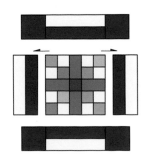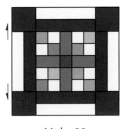

Make 20.

Assembling and Finishing

1. Sew light brown 2" x 14" sashing rectangles to the right side of all 20 blocks. Press the seam allowances toward the light brown rectangles. Sew sashing rectangles to the left side of five of the blocks. Press the seam allowances toward the sashing.

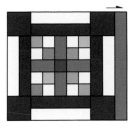

Make 15.   Make 5.

2. Sew together four light brown sashing rectangles and five rose squares as shown. Press the seam allowances toward the light brown rectangle. Make six of these sashing rows.

Make 6.

3. Arrange the blocks and sashing rows as shown. Sew the blocks into horizontal rows; press the seam allowances toward the sashing strips. Sew the rows and sashing rows together; press the seam allowances toward the sashing.

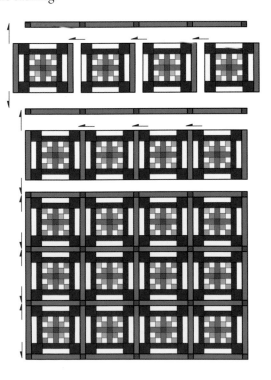

4. Referring to "Borders with Butted Corners" on page 14, measure, cut, and sew the dark brown 3½" strips to the sides of the quilt first, and then to the top and bottom.

5. Assemble the quilt sandwich and quilt as desired. Bind the edges using the rose 2½" strips; add a label. Refer to the finishing techniques beginning on page 16 in "Quiltmaking Basics" for further details as needed.

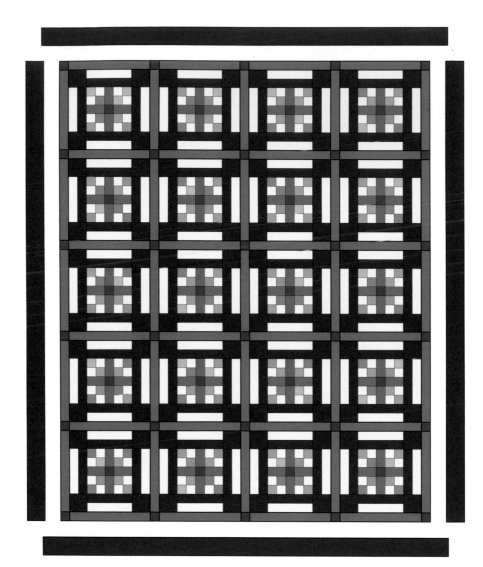

Quilt assembly

Kaleidoscope is from the Greek, meaning "beautiful forms." When I first looked at the Arrow Crown block multiplied on my computer screen, I felt like I was looking through a wonderful kaleidoscope—the cardboard tube with colored stones and paperclips in the chamber that I remember so vividly from my childhood. I accentuated that feeling by choosing bright-colored fabrics and highlighting the angles and lines with my quilting. Try making this quilt using favorite colors from your childhood.

Finished Quilt Size: 56" x 68"
Finished Block Size: 12" x 12" (20 total)

Materials

Yardages are based on 42"-wide fabric unless otherwise noted.

2⅜ yards of white fabric for blocks

¼ yard *each* (2 yards *total*) of 8 assorted colored fabrics for blocks

1⅞ yards of green fabric for blocks and inner border

1⅓ yards of blue fabric for blocks

⅞ yard of purple fabric for outer border

⅝ yard of light blue fabric for binding

3½ yards *or* 1¾ yards of 108"-wide fabric for backing

60" x 72" piece of batting

6" Bias Square ruler

Cutting

All measurements include ¼"-wide seam allowances.

From the green fabric, cut:

13 strips, 3" x 42"; cut into 160 squares, 3" x 3"

4 strips, 2" x 42"; cut into 80 squares, 2" x 2"

7 strips, 1¼" x 42"

From the white fabric, cut:

7 strips, 3" x 42"; cut into 80 squares, 3" x 3"

4 strips, 2" x 42"; cut into 80 squares, 2" x 2"

5 strips, 4¾" x 42"; cut into 40 squares, 4¾" x 4¾"

6 strips, 2⅝" x 42"; cut into 80 squares, 2⅝" x 2⅝"

2 strips, 3½" x 42"; cut into 20 squares, 3½" x 3½"

From *each* of the assorted colored fabrics, cut:

10 squares, 3" x 3" (80 total)

5 squares, 4¾" x 4¾" (40 total)

From the blue fabric, cut:

12 strips, 2" x 42"; cut into 240 squares, 2" x 2"

3 strips, 4½" x 42"; cut into 20 squares, 4½" x 4½"

From the purple fabric, cut:

7 strips, 3½" x 42"

From the light blue fabric, cut:

7 strips, 2½" x 42"

Assembling the Blocks

1. Referring to "Half-Square-Triangle Units" on page 10 and using 80 green and 80 white 3" squares, make 160 half-square-triangle units. Make another 160 half-square-triangle units using the remaining green and colored 3" squares. Press the seam allowances toward the green fabric. Trim the squares to 2". Keep the colored/green half-square-triangle units separated by the eight color groups.

Make 160 of each.

2. Sew the white 2" squares to the left side of the green/white half-square-triangle units. Sew 80 blue 2" squares to the right side as shown. Press toward the unpieced squares.

Make 80.

3. Sew a green/white half-square-triangle unit to the left side of 80 blue 2" squares as shown. Press the seam allowances toward the blue squares.

Make 80.

4. Sew green/colored half-square-triangle units from four of the eight colors to the blue side of the units from step 3 as shown. Press the seam allowances toward the blue squares.

Make 80.

5. Sew the remaining green/colored half-square-triangle units between 80 blue and 80 green 2" squares as shown. Press the seam allowances toward the unpieced squares.

Make 80.

6. Arrange the units from steps 2, 4, and 5 as shown so that the blue squares form a diagonal line from corner to corner. Determine which color groups you want to pair and sew the rows together. These will be the corners of the blocks; there should be four groups, each with 20 identical corner sections.

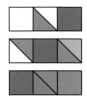

Make 80.

7. Referring to "Quarter-Square-Triangle Units" on page 11 and using the white and colored 4¾" squares, make 80 quarter-square-triangle units. To make identical blocks, sew all of the same-colored pairs together to make four groups, each with 20 identical quarter-square-triangle units. Trim the squares to 3½".

Make 80.

8. Referring to "Flying Geese" on page 13, and using the white 2⅝" squares and the blue 4½" squares, make 80 flying-geese units. Trim to 2" x 3½".

Make 80.

9. Sew the flying-geese units to a white side of the quarter-square-triangle units as shown; press.

10. Sew corner sections to opposite sides of two groups of 20 each of flying-geese units from step 9 as shown. Press the seam allowances toward the corner sections.

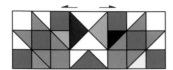

11. Sew the remaining 40 flying-geese units from step 9 to opposite sides of the white 3½" squares as shown. Press the seam allowances toward the center.

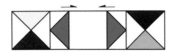

12. Sew the sections from step 10 to the center section from step 11. Press the seam allowances toward the top and bottom.

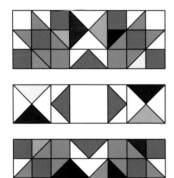

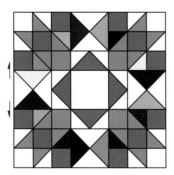

Make 20.

Assembling and Finishing

1. Arrange the blocks in five rows of four blocks each as shown. Sew the blocks into horizontal rows; press the seam allowances in opposite direction from row to row. Sew the rows together; press the seam allowances in one direction.

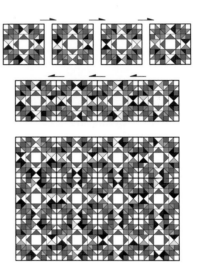

2. Referring to "Borders with Butted Corners" on page 14, measure, cut, and sew the green 1¼" inner-border strips to the sides of the quilt, and then to the top and bottom. Repeat with the purple 3½" border strips.

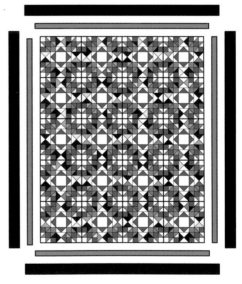

Quilt assembly

3. Assemble the quilt sandwich and quilt as desired. Bind the edges using the light blue 2½" strips; add a label. Refer to the finishing techniques beginning on page 16 in "Quiltmaking Basics" for further details as needed.

I began collecting penguins when I was in college, and over the past 20-plus years I have gathered more than a few. Usually my penguins come out around Christmas time and are put away when the January blahs turn my thoughts to spring.

   This quilt features the Mother's Fancy block. The square at the center of the star is the perfect place to highlight a cute penguin fabric, and there is enough visual interest in the quilt that the penguins don't dominate. Finally, penguins I can live with all year long! (You can easily replace the penguins with your favorite subject.)

Finished Quilt Size: 67½" x 82½"
Finished Block Size: 14" x 14" (20 total)

Materials

Yardages are based on 42"-wide fabric unless otherwise noted.

4½ yards of cream fabric for blocks and sashing

3½ yards of blue fabric for blocks, sashing squares, and outer border

⅝ yard of penguin print or other theme print for blocks and border corner squares*

½ yard of red fabric for inner border

⅔ yard of purple fabric for binding

5 yards *or* 2 yards of 108"-wide fabric for backing

72" x 87" piece of batting

6" Bias Square ruler

*Additional fabric will be required for fussy cutting block centers. Refer to "Determining Yardage for Fussy Cutting" on page 9 for details on estimating yardage.

Cutting

All measurements include ¼"-wide seam allowances.

From the cream fabric, cut:

8 strips, 3½" x 42"; cut into 80 squares, 3½" x 3½"

5 strips, 2½" x 42"; cut into 80 squares, 2½" x 2½"

40 strips, 1½" x 42"; cut into 160 rectangles, 1½" x 8½"

13 strips, 1½" x 42"; cut into 320 squares, 1½" x 1½"

16 strips, 1½" x 42"; cut into 31 strips, 1½" x 14½"

From the blue fabric, cut:

8 strips, 3½" x 42"; cut into 80 squares, 3½" x 3½"

20 strips, 1½" x 42"; cut into 80 rectangles, 1½" x 8½"

17 strips, 1½" x 42"; cut into 412 squares, 1½" x 1½"

8 strips, 3½" x 42"

From the penguin print, cut:

20 squares, 4½" x 4½"

4 squares, 3½" x 3½"

From the red fabric, cut:

8 strips, 1½" x 42"

From the purple fabric, cut:

8 strips, 2½" x 42"

Assembling the Blocks

1. Referring to "Half-Square-Triangle Units" on page 10 and using the cream and blue 3½" squares, make 160 half-square-triangle units. Press the seam allowances of half of the completed units toward the blue fabric and the seam allowances of the other half toward the cream fabric. Trim squares to 2½".

Make 80 of each.

2. Pair a half-square-triangle unit pressed toward the blue fabric with one pressed toward the cream fabric and sew the units together so that the cream sections form a V. The seams should butt together for easy alignment and sharp points. Press; repeat to make 80 star points total.

Make 80.

3. Sew 40 star points to opposite sides of the penguin print 4½" squares so that the cream point of the V is touching the center square. Press the seam allowances toward the penguin fabric.

4. Sew the cream 2½" squares to opposite sides of the 40 remaining star points; press the seam allowances toward the cream fabric.

Make 40.

5. Sew the star-point units from step 4 to the top and bottom of the center section from step 3 as shown; press the seam allowances toward the penguin fabric. Make 20 Star blocks.

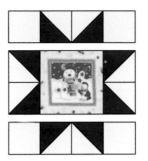 

Make 20.

6. Sew the cream 1½" x 8½" rectangles to opposite sides of the blue rectangles. Press the seam allowances toward the blue rectangles, being careful to avoid distorting the pieces.

7. Sew blue and cream 1½" squares together as shown to make a nine-patch unit. Make 80. (There will be 12 blue squares remaining.)

Make 80.

8. Sew the nine-patch units to opposite sides of 40 of the units from step 6 and press the seam allowances toward the rectangles.

9. Sew the remaining units from step 6 to opposite sides of the 20 Star blocks and press the seam allowances toward the rectangle strips.

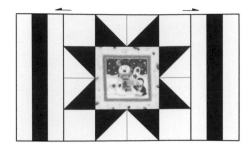

10. Sew the units from step 8 to the top and bottom of the Star blocks to complete the blocks. Press the seam allowances toward the top and bottom. Make 20 blocks.

Make 20.

Assembling and Finishing

1. Sew a cream 1½" x 14½" sashing strip to one side of 19 blocks. Press the seam allowances toward the sashing strips.

2. Sew blue 1½" squares onto one end of the remaining 12 cream 1½" x 14½" sashing strips. Press the seam allowances toward the sashing strips.

3. Sew the sashing strips with squares to the bottom edge of 12 of the blocks with sashing on the side.

4. Arrange the blocks as shown. Sew the blocks into horizontal rows; press the seam allowances toward the sashing strips. Sew the rows together; press the seam allowances toward the sashing.

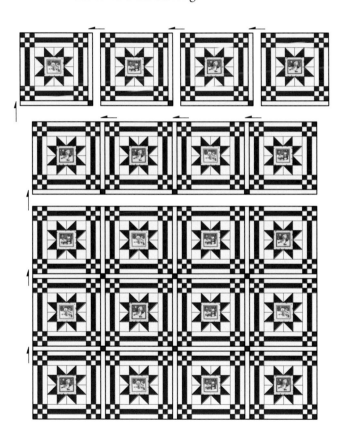

5. Referring to "Borders with Butted Corners" on page 14, measure, cut, and sew the red 1½" inner-border strips to the sides of the quilt, and then to the top and bottom.

6. Referring to "Borders with Corner Squares" on page 14, measure and trim the blue 3½" border strips to the determined length, piecing as necessary. Sew the side border strips to the sides of the quilt. Sew the penguin print 3½" squares to each end of the top and bottom border strips, and then sew the border strips to the top and bottom of the quilt, making sure that the penguins will be right side up in the completed top.

7. Assemble the quilt sandwich and quilt as desired. Bind the edges using the purple 2½" strips; add a label. Refer to the finishing techniques beginning on page 16 in "Quiltmaking Basics" for further details as needed.

Quilt assembly

An Afternoon Nap

Nine blocks, set three by three and sewn into a baby quilt, would make a wonderful baby gift. And what could be more appropriate for a new baby than a quilt made from a block called Mother's Fancy!

To make a 44" x 44" version of "Karin's Fancy," you will need:
2¼ yards of cream fabric for blocks and sashing
1¼ yards of green fabric for blocks, sashing squares, and binding
½ yard *total* of assorted colored fabrics for blocks
⅜ yard or more of theme print*
2⅝ yards of fabric for backing
46" x 46" piece of batting

*Refer to "Determining Yardage for Fussy Cutting" on page 9 if you will be fussy cutting your fabric.

From the cream fabric, cut:
4 strips, 3½" x 42"; cut into 36 squares, 3½" x 3½"
3 strips, 2½" x 42", cut into 36 squares, 2½" x 2½"
18 strips, 1½" x 42", cut into 72 rectangles, 1½" x 8½"
6 strips, 1½" x 42", cut into 144 squares, 1½" x 1½"
6 strips, 1½" x 42", cut into 12 strips, 1½" x 14½"

From the assorted colored fabrics, cut:
4 strips, 3½" x 42"; cut into 36 squares, 3½" x 3½"

From the green fabric, cut:
9 strips, 1½" x 42"; cut into 36 rectangles, 1½" x 8½"
8 strips, 1½" x 42"; cut into 184 squares, 1½" x 1½"
5 strips, 2½" x 42"

From the theme print, cut:
9 squares, 4½" x 4½"

Little Boxes

I usually begin designing quilts by choosing a block that I like. Sometimes when working on the computer, the resulting quilt doesn't turn out quite the way I imagined it would. This block, called Building Blocks, was one of those cases. Usually I delete the quilt and move on, but I kept playing with this one. When I added sashing and a pieced border, the design fell into place. I am thrilled with the results! I hope you enjoy choosing fabrics and colors to create your own version of "Little Boxes."

Finished Quilt Size: 59" x 74"
Finished Block Size: 13½" x 13½" (12 total)

Materials

Yardages are based on 42"-wide fabric unless otherwise noted.

2⅜ yards of crimson fabric for blocks, sashing squares, and borders

2¼ yards of cream fabric for blocks, sashing, and pieced border

1 yard *total* of assorted colored fabrics for blocks and pieced border

⅝ yard of blue fabric for binding

3½ yards *or* 1¾ yards of 108"-wide fabric for backing

63" x 78" piece of batting

Cutting

All measurements include ¼"-wide seam allowances.

From the cream fabric, cut:

16 strips, 2" x 42"; cut into 318 squares, 2" x 2"

4 strips, 5" x 42"; cut into:
    12 squares, 5" x 5"
    48 rectangles, 2" x 5"

9 strips, 2" x 42"; cut into 17 strips, 2" x 14"

From the assorted colored fabrics, cut:

270 squares, 2" x 2"

From the crimson fabric, cut:

5 strips, 5" x 42"; cut into:
    96 rectangles, 2" x 5"
    6 squares, 2" x 2"

14 strips, 3½" x 42"

From the blue fabric, cut:

7 strips, 2½" x 42"

Assembling the Blocks

1. Sew 144 cream and colored 2" squares together into pairs. Press the seam allowances toward the colored fabric. Then sew colored 2" squares to the cream side of 48 pairs and cream squares to the colored side of the remaining 96 pairs. Press the seam allowances toward the colored fabric.

Make 48.   Make 96.

2. Sew the units from step 1 together as shown to make nine-patch units. Press the seam allowances toward the center. Make 48.

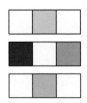

Make 48.

3. Sew the 96 crimson rectangles to each long side of the 48 cream rectangles. Press the seam allowances toward the crimson rectangles.

4. Sew nine-patch units to opposite ends of 24 of the crimson/cream units as shown; press the seam allowances toward the center.

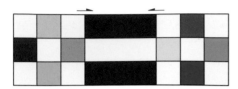

Make 24.

5. Sew a unit from step 3 to opposite sides of the cream 5" squares as shown; press the seam allowances toward the crimson rectangles.

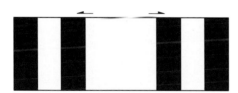

Make 12.

6. Sew the nine-patch units to the top and bottom of the center section to complete the block; press the seam allowances toward the center. Make 12 blocks.

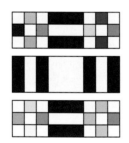
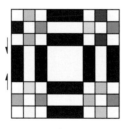

Make 12.

Assembling and Finishing

1. Sew cream 2" x 14" sashing strips onto one side of 11 of the completed blocks; press the seam allowances toward the sashing strip.

2. Sew a crimson square onto one end of each of the remaining sashing strips; press the seam allowances toward the sashing strips. Sew these strips to the bottom of six of the blocks with sashing. One block will have no sashing on it.

3. Arrange the blocks as shown. Sew the blocks into horizontal rows; press the seam allowances toward the sashing. Sew the rows together; press the seam allowances toward sashing.

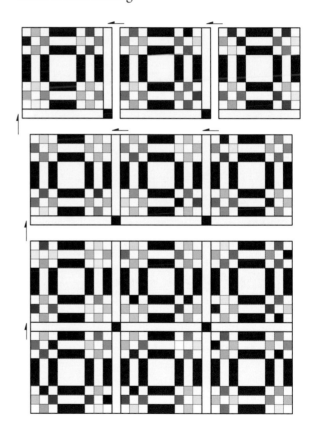

4. Referring to "Borders with Butted Corners" on page 14, measure, cut, and sew the crimson 3½" inner-border strips to the sides of the quilt, and then to the top and bottom.

5. Make the pieced borders by sewing together the cream and the colored 2" squares. For the side borders, sew 22 colored squares and 21 cream squares together, alternating them as shown; press the seam allowances toward the colored squares. For the top and bottom border, sew together 18 cream squares and 17 colored squares; press the seam allowances toward the colored squares.

Side border.
Make 2.

Top/bottom border.
Make 2.

6. Sew the borders to the sides of the quilt; press the seam allowances outward. Sew the top and bottom borders to the quilt; press the seam allowances outward.

7. Add the final crimson 3½" border in the same manner as the first one, sewing the side borders first, and then the top and bottom; press the seam allowances outward.

8. Assemble the quilt sandwich and quilt as desired. Bind the edges using the blue 2½" strips; add a label. Refer to the finishing techniques beginning on page 16 in "Quiltmaking Basics" for further details as needed.

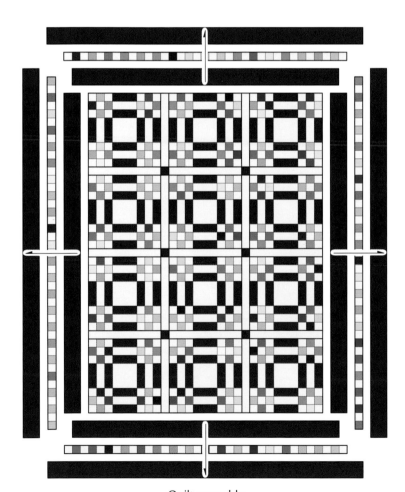

Quilt assembly

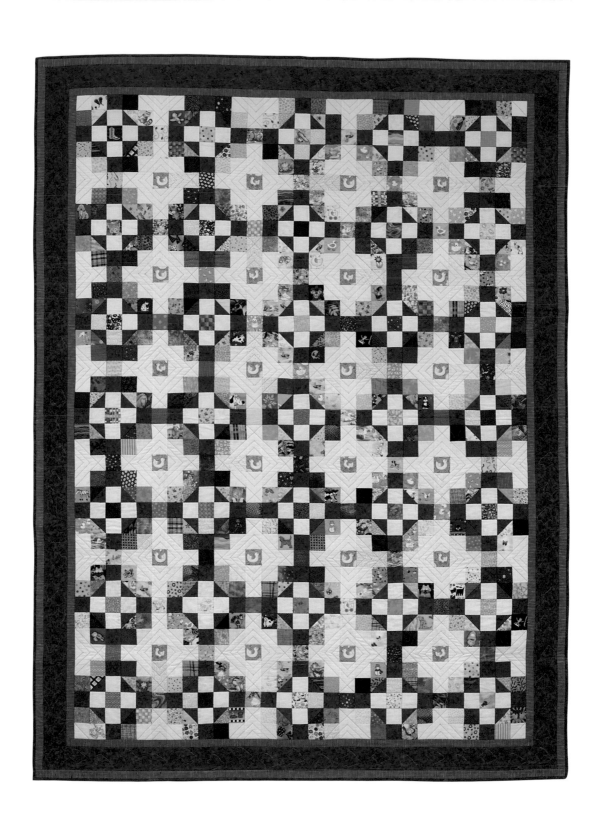

I wanted to capture in a quilt the joy that I have always felt upon reading Robert McCloskey's book, *Make Way for Ducklings*. I chose the State of Georgia block because the colored squares in the block corners were connected diagonally and I could fussy cut 2½" squares of duck fabric to create a duck trail. The block also worked well because when I added sashing and sashing squares, I could highlight ducks prominently between the blocks. I spent months going to different quilt stores collecting duck fabrics. The wandering duck trail is a subtle surprise in the quilt, and the result is even better than what I envisioned. Use any animal or print that you like. What fun!

Finished Quilt Size: 68½" x 92½"
Finished Block Size: 10" x 10" (35 total)

Materials

Yardages are based on 42"-wide fabric unless otherwise noted.

2⅝ yards *total* of assorted white and cream fabrics for blocks and sashing

2⅜ yards *total* of assorted colored fabrics for blocks and sashing

2⅜ yards of blue fabric for blocks and middle border

⅞ yard of purple fabric for inner and outer borders

⅜ yard *total* of assorted duck prints*

¼ yard of purple duck print for sashing squares*

¾ yard of dark purple fabric for binding

5½ yards *or* 2 yards of 108"-wide fabric for backing

73" x 97" piece of batting

6" Bias Square ruler

*Additional fabric will be required if fussy cutting the squares for the blocks and sashing. Refer to "Determining Yardage for Fussy Cutting" on page 9 for details on estimating yardage. I purchased ¼-yard cuts of several different duck prints for this quilt. You can make the duck trail using just one duck print if you like.

Cutting

All measurements include ¼"-wide seam allowances.

From the blue fabric, cut:

15 strips, 3½" x 42"; cut 7 of the strips into 70 squares, 3½" x 3½"

9 strips, 2½" x 42"; cut into 140 squares, 2½" x 2½"

From the assorted colored fabrics, cut:

70 squares, 3½" x 3½"

314 squares, 2½" x 2 ½"

From the assorted duck prints, cut:

59 squares, 2½" x 2½"

From the assorted white and cream fabrics, cut:

280 squares, 2½" x 2½"

116 rectangles, 2½" x 4½"

From the purple duck print, cut:

24 squares, 2½" x 2½"

From the purple fabric, cut:

17 strips, 1½" x 42"

From the dark purple fabric, cut:

9 strips, 2½" x 42"

Assembling the Blocks

1. Referring to "Half-Square-Triangle Units" on page 10 and using the blue and colored 3½" squares, make 140 half-square-triangle units. Press the seam allowances toward the blue fabric. Trim the squares to 2½".

2. Sew 120 colored and 20 duck print 2½" squares to the half-square-triangle units. To ensure that the duck print squares are oriented correctly in the finished block (standing on their feet and not their heads), be sure to position the duck squares as shown. Press the seam allowances toward the unpieced squares.

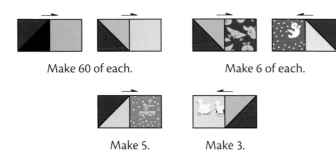

Make 60 of each.   Make 6 of each.

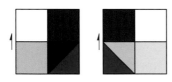

Make 5.   Make 3.

3. Sew 120 colored and 20 duck print 2½" squares to 140 of the white 2½" squares. Sew duck print squares to the left side of 11 of the white squares and to the right side of 9 of the white squares. Be sure the ducks are oriented as shown. Press the seam allowances toward the colored and duck print squares.

Make 120.   Make 11.   Make 9.

4. Set aside the 40 duck print units. Sew units from steps 2 and 3 together as shown to make the corner sections of the blocks; press the seam allowances toward the white squares.

Make 60 of each.

5. Sew the duck print units from step 2 and 3 into pairs as indicated. Be sure the ducks are oriented correctly in each of the corner sections.

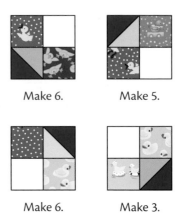

Make 6.   Make 5.

Make 6.   Make 3.

6. Sew the blue 2½" squares to the remaining white 2½" squares; press the seam allowances toward the white squares.

Make 140.

7. Sew the corner sections to opposite sides of 70 blue/white units from step 6 as shown. Make 51 using colored squares and 19 using duck print squares; press the seam allowances toward the blue/white units. The yellow squares in the illustrations indicate duck prints in the 19 units.

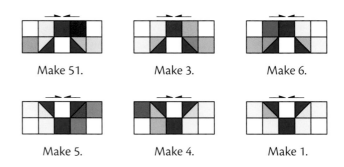

Make 51.   Make 3.   Make 6.

Make 5.   Make 4.   Make 1.

8. Sew the remaining blue/white units to 35 of the remaining colored 2½" squares as shown; press the seam allowances toward the white squares.

Make 35.

9. Sew the top and bottom sections without duck print fabrics to the top and bottom of the center strip, aligning seams. Make sure that the blue segment of the half-square-triangle unit abuts the white section of the center strip. Press the seam allowances toward the center. Make 19 blocks.

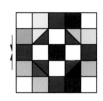

Make 19.

10. Assemble the duck print blocks as shown. You'll have 16 blocks with duck prints.

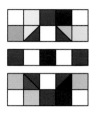

Make 4.   Make 4.

Make 2.   Make 2.   Make 2.

Make 1.   Make 1.

Assembling and Finishing

1. To make the sashing, sew the white rectangles to opposite sides of the remaining colored 2½" squares. Make 39 sashing units with colored squares; press the seam allowances toward the white rectangles. Sew white rectangles to the sides of 10 of the assorted duck print squares and to the top and bottom edges of 9 of the assorted duck print squares to make 19 sashing units with duck print squares. Press toward the white rectangles.

2. Arrange the blocks, colored sashing, and purple duck print squares in rows as shown. Make sure the duck prints are all oriented correctly. Sew the rows together; press the seam allowances toward the sashing.

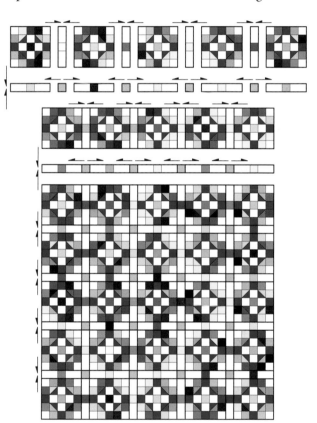

3. Sew the rows together and press the seam allowances toward the sashing rows.

4. Referring to "Borders with Butted Corners" on page 14, measure, cut, and sew the purple 1½" inner-border strips to the sides of the quilt first, and then to the top and bottom. Repeat for the blue 3½" center-border strips and the purple 1½" outer-border strips.

5. Assemble the quilt sandwich and quilt as desired. Use the duck print quilting design at right in the border if you like. Bind the edges using the dark purple 2½" strips; add a label. Refer to the finishing techniques beginning on page 16 in "Quiltmaking Basics" for further details as needed.

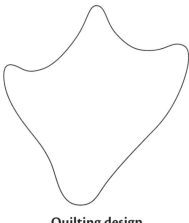

Quilting design

Quilt assembly

When I was designing this quilt on the computer using the Swamp Angel block, my husband, Matt, really connected with it. He is attracted to architectural motifs and felt that the green triangles in the center section created the look of mosaic tiles. I liked it, but felt it needed something more, so I added a pieced border. The bright colors in the pieced border provide a nice frame for the tiling and balance out the overall design. Of course, if green isn't your color, any other color will be fabulous as well.

Finished Quilt Size: 66½" x 75½"
Finished Block Size: 9" x 9" (42 total)

Materials

Yardages are based on 42"-wide fabric unless otherwise noted.

4⅜ yards of white fabric for blocks and pieced border

2½ yards of green fabric for blocks and borders

2⅛ yards *total* of assorted colored fabrics for blocks and pieced border

⅝ yard of blue fabric for binding

4½ yards *or* 2 yards of 108"-wide fabric for backing

71" x 80" piece of batting

6" Bias Square ruler

Cutting

All measurements include ¼"-wide seam allowances.

From the green fabric, cut:

11 strips, 4½" x 42"; cut into 84 squares, 4½" x 4½"

15 strips, 2" x 42"

From the white fabric, cut:

11 strips, 4½" x 42"; cut into 84 squares, 4½" x 4½"

11 strips, 4¾" x 42"; cut into 84 squares, 4¾" x 4¾"

4 strips, 3½" x 42"; cut into 42 squares, 3½" x 3½"

8 squares, 2⅜" x 2⅜"; cut once diagonally to make 16 half-square triangles

5 strips, 4¼" x 42"; cut into 41 squares, 4¼" x 4¼". Cut the squares twice diagonally to make 164 quarter-square triangles.

From the assorted colored fabrics, cut:

84 squares, 4¾" x 4¾"

86 squares, 2⅝" x 2⅝"

From the blue fabric, cut:

8 strips, 2½" x 42"

Assembling the Blocks

1. Referring to "Half-Square-Triangle Units" on page 10 and using the green and white 4½" squares, assemble 168 half-square-triangle units. Press the seam allowances toward the green fabric and trim the squares to 3½".

2. Referring to "Quarter-Square-Triangle Units" on page 11 and using the colored and white 4¾" squares, make 168 quarter-square-triangle units. Press the seam allowances toward the colored fabric and trim the squares to 3½".

Make 168.

3. Sew the green side of the half-square-triangle units to the white sides of 84 quarter-square-triangle units as shown to make the top and bottom sections of the blocks; press the seam allowances toward the half-square-triangle units.

4. Sew the remaining quarter-square-triangle units to opposite sides of the white 3½" squares as shown to make the center of the block; press the seam allowances toward the center squares.

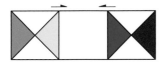

5. Sew the top and bottom units from step 3 to the center units from step 4; press. Make 42 blocks.

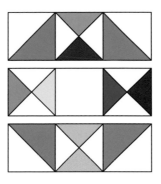 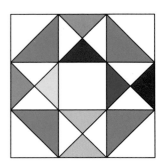

Make 42.

Assembling and Finishing

1. Arrange the blocks in seven rows of six blocks each as shown. Sew the blocks into horizontal rows; press the seam allowances in opposite direction from row to row. Sew the rows together; press the seam allowances in one direction.

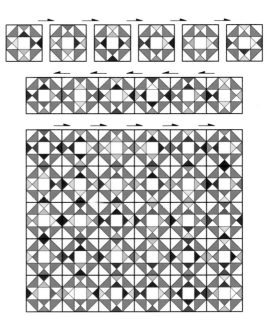

2. Referring to "Borders with Butted Corners" on page 14, measure, cut, and sew the green 2" inner-border strips to the sides of the quilt, and then to the top and bottom.

3. Center and sew the long side of two white 2⅜" triangles to adjacent sides of eight colored 2⅝" squares. Press the seam allowances toward the white fabric.

Make 8.

4. Sew the short side of a white 4¼" triangle to the upper-right side of the units from step 3. Press the seam allowances toward the white triangles. Set aside for the ends of the borders.

Make 8.

5. Sew the short side of the remaining white 4¼" triangles to two opposite sides of the remaining colored 2⅝" squares as shown. Press toward the white triangles. The white triangles will extend beyond the assorted squares.

Make 78.

6. Sew the border sections from step 5 together into two strips of 20 sections each for the side borders and two strips of 19 sections each for the top and bottom. The points of the colored squares should line up.

Side border.
Make 2.

Top/bottom border.
Make 2.

7. Sew an end section from step 4 to each end of the border strips. Sew the longer borders to the sides of the quilt; press toward the inner border. Sew the top and bottom borders to the quilt; press.

8. Following the directions for "Borders with Butted Corners" on page 14, measure, cut, and sew the green 2" outer-border strips to the sides of the quilt, and then to the top and bottom.

Quilt assembly

9. Assemble the quilt sandwich and quilt as desired. Bind the edges using the blue 2½" strips; add a label. Refer to the finishing techniques beginning on page 16 in "Quiltmaking Basics" for further details as needed.

Puss in the Corner . . . Mice on the Run

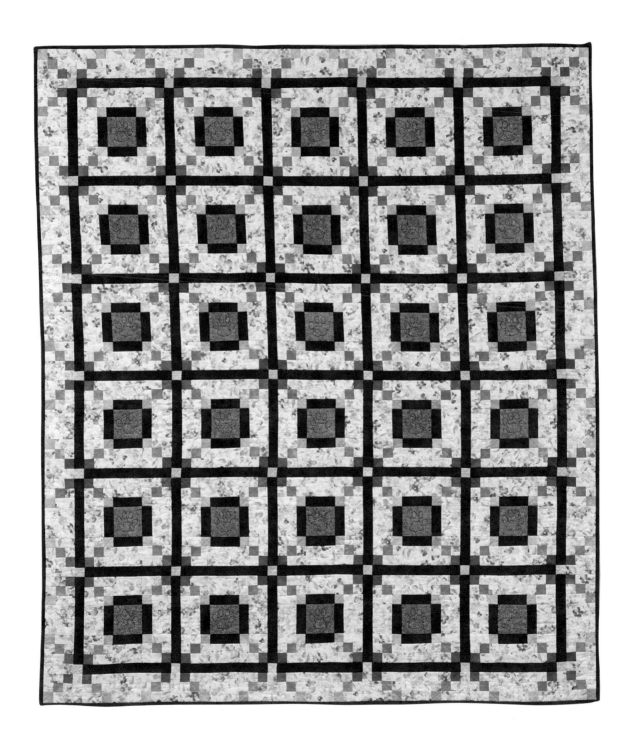

When I saw the name of the block Puss in the Corner, the rest of the title immediately jumped into my head. I initially considered making a quilt that was all cat and mouse fabric, but then decided that I wanted it to be subtle. I chose fabric that was soft and flowing and had nothing to do with cats or mice. Instead, I used the theme in the quilting itself. It took 142 mice, 51 paw prints, and one cat to complete the free-motion quilting, but it was worth it!

Finished Quilt Size: 57½" x 67½"
Finished Blocks Size: 9" x 9" (30 total)

Materials

Yardages are based on 42"-wide fabric unless otherwise noted.

2⅞ yards of yellow floral for blocks and border

1⅞ yards of fuchsia fabric for blocks, sashing, and binding

⅜ yard *each* of light, medium, and dark green fabric for blocks and border

⅜ yard of pink fabric for blocks

⅛ yard of very light green fabric for sashing

3½ yards *or* 1¾ yards of 108"-wide fabric for backing

62" x 72" piece of batting

Hand-Dyed Fabrics

I hand dyed fabric for the four different shades of green. Hand-dyed fabric is available at quilt stores and online, but it's a lot of fun to dye your own. I used *Hand-Dyed Fabric Made Easy* by Adriene Buffington (That Patchwork Place, 1996). This book makes it a simple process to create hand-dyed fabric.

Cutting

All measurements include ¼"-wide seam allowances.

From the light green fabric, cut:

7 strips, 1½" x 42"; cut into 168 squares, 1½" x 1½"

From the yellow floral, cut:

38 strips, 1½" x 42"; cut into:
- 336 rectangles, 1½" x 2½"
- 336 squares, 1½" x 1½"
- 26 rectangles, 1½" x 3½"

11 strips, 2½" x 42"; cut into 120 rectangles, 2½" x 3½"

2 strips, 3½" x 42"; cut into 22 squares, 3½" x 3½"

From the dark green fabric, cut:

7 strips, 1½" x 42"; cut into 168 squares, 1½" x 1½"

From the medium green fabric, cut:

7 strips, 1½" x 42"; cut into 168 squares, 1½" x 1½"

From the fuchsia fabric, cut:

29 strips, 1½" x 42"; cut into:
- 120 rectangles, 1½" x 3½"
- 71 strips, 1½" x 9½"

7 strips, 2½" x 42"

From the pink fabric, cut:

3 strips, 3½" x 42"; cut into 30 squares, 3½" x 3½"

From the very light green fabric, cut:

2 strips, 1½" x 42"; cut into 42 squares, 1½" x 1½"

Assembling the Blocks

1. Sew the light green squares to 168 of the floral 1½" x 2½" rectangles. Sew the dark green squares to the remaining floral 1½" x 2½" rectangles. Press the seam allowances toward the green squares.

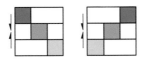

Make 168 of each.

2. Sew floral 1½" squares to opposite sides of the medium green squares. Press the seam allowances toward the green squares.

Make 168.

3. Sew the light green, medium green, and dark green segments together as shown to make 84 of each. Press the seam allowances toward the center sections. Set aside 24 of each to use later in the pieced border.

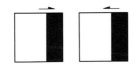

Make 84 of each.

4. Sew the fuchsia 1½" x 3½" rectangles to the floral 2½" x 3½" rectangles. Press the seam allowances toward the fuchsia fabric in 60 units and toward the floral in the other 60 units.

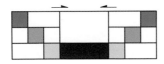

Make 60 of each.

5. Sew 60 of the units from step 3 to opposite sides of the fuchsia/floral units from step 4 that were pressed toward the fuchsia. Press the seam allowances toward the center section.

Make 60.

6. Sew the remaining floral and fuchsia units from step 4 to opposite sides of the pink squares. Press the seam allowances toward the fuchsia rectangles.

Make 30.

7. Sew the top and bottom sections from step 5 to the center section from step 6; press the seam allowances toward the center. Make 30 blocks.

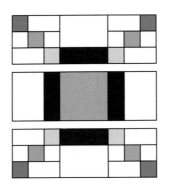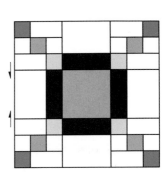

Make 30.

Assembling and Finishing

1. Sew fuchsia 1½" x 9½" sashing strips to one side of all of the completed blocks. Press the seam allowances toward the sashing strips. Then sew sashing strips to the opposite side of six of the completed blocks; press the seam allowances toward the sashing strips.

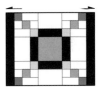

Make 24.   Make 6.

2. Sew sashing rows using the very light green squares and the fuchsia 1½" x 9½" sashing strips. Make seven rows with five fuchsia sashing pieces and six green squares in each; press the seam allowances toward the sashing strips.

Make 7.

3. Arrange the blocks and sashing rows as shown. Sew the blocks into horizontal rows; press toward the sashing strips. Sew the block and sashing rows together; press the seam allowances toward the sashing rows.

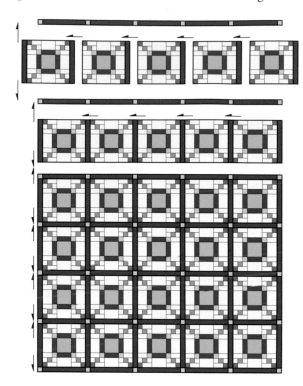

4. Make the pieced borders by sewing the remaining pieced units to floral 3½" squares and floral 1½" x 3½" rectangles as shown. Make two with 12 pieced blocks, six squares, and seven rectangles for the side borders. Make two with 12 pieced blocks, five squares, and six rectangles for the top and bottom. Press the seam allowances toward the squares and rectangles.

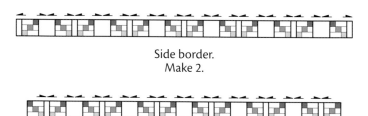

Side border.
Make 2.

Top/bottom border.
Make 2.

5. Sew the side borders onto the quilt, carefully matching seams. The green squares should continue the Xs from the quilt top. Press the seam allowances toward the border.

6. Sew the top and bottom borders onto the quilt, carefully aligning the seams. Press the seam allowances toward the border.

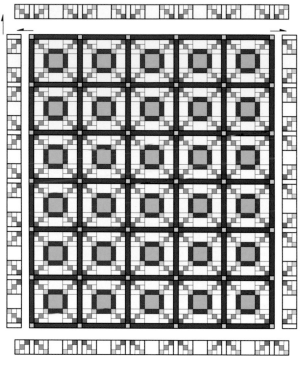

Quilt assembly

7. Assemble the quilt sandwich and quilt as desired. Use the cat and paw print quilting designs on page 73 in the borders and scattered around the quilt if desired. The mouse quilting design is a copyrighted pattern, so it can't be included. Try your hand at sketching a mouse of your own to fit inside the rectangles of the block. Bind the edges using the fuchsia 2½" strips; add a label. Refer to the finishing techniques beginning on page 16 in "Quiltmaking Basics" for further details as needed.

Quilting designs

The Raspberry Thief

This quilt is a vivid reminder of many wonderful childhood summers. The summer when I was two years old, I got lost. My mother turned her back for a second, and I was gone. After checking the house, the front yard, and the neighbors' yards, she finally found me in the middle of the raspberry patch in our backyard. I was stuck, but happily eating all the berries I could reach. Many years have passed, and I am still the one to find the first raspberries in the spring and the final berries of late summer. When I found the berry print fabrics, I knew a special quilt was in order. I used the Maple Star block.

Finished Quilt Size: 59½" x 71½"
Finished Block Size: 9" x 9" (20 total)

Materials

Yardages are based on 42"-wide fabric unless otherwise noted.

3⅛ yards of white fabric for blocks, sashing, and pieced inner border

1½ yards *total* of assorted colored fabrics for blocks, sashing, and pieced inner border

1½ yards of raspberry print for blocks, sashing squares, and border

¼ yard of blueberry print for blocks

⅝ yard of green fabric for binding

3⅝ yards *or* 1⅞ yards of 108"-wide fabric for backing

64" x 76" piece of batting

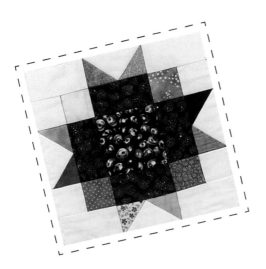

Cutting

All measurements include ¼"-wide seam allowances.

From the white fabric, cut:

4 strips, 4½" x 42"; cut into 26 squares, 4½" x 4½"

17 strips, 2" x 42"; cut into:

    84 squares, 2" x 2"

    80 rectangles, 2" x 3½"

    18 rectangles, 2" x 9½"

13 strips, 3½" x 42"; cut into 49 rectangles, 3½" x 9½"

From the assorted colored fabrics, cut:

104 squares, 2⅝" x 2⅝"

276 squares, 2" x 2"

From the raspberry print, cut:

7 strips, 3½" x 42"; cut into:

    30 squares, 3½" x 3½"

    80 rectangles, 2" x 3½"

7 strips, 3" x 42"

From the blueberry print, cut:

2 strips, 3½" x 42"; cut into 20 squares, 3½" x 3½"

From the green fabric, cut:

7 strips, 2½" x 42"

Assembling the Blocks

1. Referring to "Flying Geese" on page 13 and using the white 4½" squares and the colored 2⅝" squares, assemble 104 flying-geese units. Trim the units to 2" x 3½".

Make 104.

2. Sew the raspberry 2" x 3½" rectangles to the colored edge of 80 flying-geese units. Press the seam allowances toward the rectangles. Set aside the remaining flying-geese units for use in the pieced inner border.

Make 80.

3. Sew 80 white 2" squares to 80 colored 2" squares. Press the seam allowances toward the white squares.

Make 80.

4. Sew a white 2" x 3½" rectangle to each of the units from step 3 as shown. Make 40 with the colored square on the right and 40 with the colored square on the left. Press the seam allowances toward the colored square.

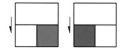

Make 40 of each.

5. Arrange the units from step 4, the flying-geese units, and the blueberry squares in rows as shown. Press the seam allowances in the direction indicated by the arrows. Sew the units into rows and sew the rows together to make the block. Make 20 blocks.

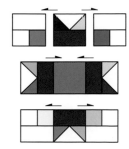

Make 20.

Assembling and Finishing

1. Draw a diagonal line from corner to corner on the wrong side of the remaining colored 2" squares. Align the assorted square with the corner of a white 3½" x 9½" rectangle as shown. Sew on the drawn line and trim the excess fabric, leaving a ¼" seam allowance. Press the seam allowances toward the corner.

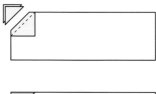

2. Repeat for the remaining corners on all of the white rectangles to make 49 sashing units; press the seam allowances toward the corners.

Make 49.

3. Sew sashing units to one side of all of the completed blocks. Press the seam allowances toward the sashing. Sew sashing units to the opposite side of five of the completed blocks. Press the seam allowances toward the sashing.

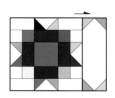
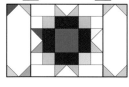

Make 15.   Make 5.

4. Sew five raspberry squares and four sashing units together to make a sashing row. Press the seam allowances toward the sashing units. Make six rows.

Make 6.

5. Arrange the blocks and sashing rows as shown. Sew the blocks into horizontal rows; press toward the sashing units. Sew the rows together; press the seam allowances toward the sashing rows.

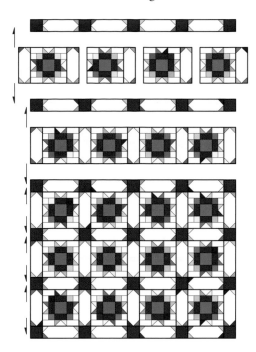

6. Sew six flying-geese units to five white 2" x 9½" rectangles as shown to make each of the pieced side borders. Sew five flying-geese units to four white rectangles for the top and bottom borders. Sew a white 2" square to each end. Press the seam allowances toward the flying-geese units. (You will have two extra flying-geese units.)

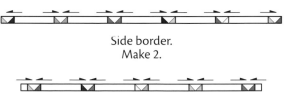

Side border.
Make 2.

Top/bottom border.
Make 2.

7. Sew the borders to the sides of the quilt, carefully aligning the flying-geese units with the sashing squares to complete the stars. Press the seam allowances outward.

8. Sew the top and bottom borders to the quilt. Press the seam allowances outward.

9. Referring to "Borders with Butted Corners" on page 14, measure, cut, and sew the raspberry 3" border strips to the sides of the quilt, and then to the top and bottom.

Quilt assembly

10. Assemble the quilt sandwich and quilt as desired. Use the footprint quilting design below in the sashing. Bind the edges using the green 2½" strips; add a label. Refer to the finishing techniques beginning on page 16 in "Quiltmaking Basics" for further details as needed.

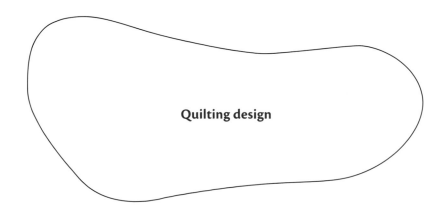

Quilting design

Shazam!

I like bright colorful quilts. I don't believe that bright colors are only for children's quilts, or that adult quilts can't be fun. What appealed to me immediately when I was designing this quilt was the potential for color! And extending the flying-geese points into the border produces an added element of fun, like an exploding firework bursting out into the world. Ironically, the block is called Snowy Owl. Here's your chance to go for a riot of color—either for yourself or as a cheerful gift.

Finished Quilt Size: 68½" x 80½"
Finished Block Size: 12" x 12" (30 total)

Materials

Yardages are based on 42"-wide fabric unless otherwise noted.

3⅝ yards *total* of assorted colored fabrics for blocks

3¼ yards of white fabric for blocks

1⅜ yards of purple fabric for borders

⅔ yard of red fabric for binding

5 yards *or* 2⅛ yards of 108"-wide fabric for backing

73" x 85" piece of batting

Cutting

All measurements include ¼"-wide seam allowances.

From the assorted colored fabrics, cut:

120 squares, 2½" x 2½"

60 rectangles, 4½" x 5½"

66 squares, 5½" x 5½"

From the white fabric, cut:

11 strips, 2½" x 42"; cut into 120 rectangles, 2½" x 3½"

19 strips, 3" x 42"; cut into 240 squares, 3" x 3"

4 strips, 4½" x 42"; cut into 30 squares, 4½" x 4½"

From the purple fabric, cut:

2 strips, 3" x 42"; cut into 24 squares, 3" x 3"

6 strips, 2½" x 42"; cut into:

    18 rectangles, 2½" x 8½"

    4 rectangles, 2½" x 4½"

    4 rectangles, 2½" x 6½"

8 strips, 2½" x 42"

From the red fabric, cut:

8 strips, 2½" x 42"

Assembling the Blocks

1. Referring to "Mary's Triangles Blocks" on page 12 and using the colored 2½" squares, the white rectangles, and the colored rectangles, make 120 blocks. The completed blocks should measure 4½".

Make 120.

2. Referring to "Flying Geese" on page 13 and using the white 3" squares and 60 of the colored 5½" squares, make 240 flying-geese units. Using the six remaining colored 5½" squares and the purple 3" squares, make 24 flying-geese units to be used in the border. Trim all the flying-geese units to 2½" x 4½".

Make 240.   Make 24.

3. Sew the white flying-geese units together in pairs, one on top of the other as shown. Press the seam allowances toward the upper flying-geese units.

Make 120.

4. Sew completed Mary's Triangles blocks to opposite sides of 60 of the flying-geese pairs. The small squares in the Mary's Triangles blocks should be next to the flying-geese pairs. Press the seam allowances toward the Mary's Triangles blocks.

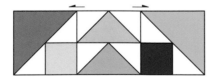

5. Sew the remaining flying-geese pairs to opposite sides of the white 4½" squares. The flying geese should point away from the center square. Press the seam allowances toward the white square.

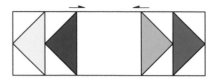

6. Sew the Mary's triangles sections to the top and bottom of the center section. All of the flying geese should point away from the center square. Press the seam allowances toward the center section. Make 30 blocks.

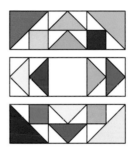 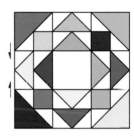

Make 30.

Assembling and Finishing

1. Arrange the blocks in six rows of five blocks each. Sew the blocks into horizontal rows; press the seam allowances in opposite directions from row to row. Sew the rows together; press in one direction.

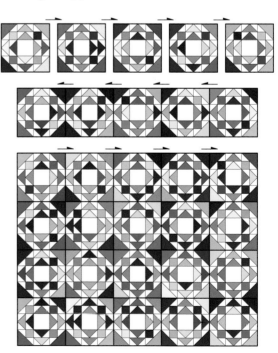

2. Sew six flying-geese units with purple corners to five purple 2½" x 8½" rectangles. The flying-geese units should all be pointing the same direction. Sew a purple 2½" x 4½" rectangle to each end to make a side border. Press toward the flying-geese units. Make two.

Side border.
Make 2.

3. Sew five flying-geese units to four purple 2½" x 8½" rectangles. Sew a purple 2½" x 6½" rectangle to each end. Make two for the top and bottom borders.

Top/bottom border.
Make 2.

4. Sew the borders from step 2 to the sides of the quilt, carefully aligning the flying geese in the border with those along the edge of the quilt. Press the seam allowances toward the border. Sew the borders from step 3 to the top and bottom of the quilt; press.

5. Referring to "Borders with Butted Corners" on page 14, measure, cut, and sew the purple 2½" border strips to the sides of the quilt, and then to the top and bottom.

6. Assemble the quilt sandwich and quilt as desired. Bind the edges using the red 2½" strips; add a label. Refer to the finishing techniques beginning on page 16 in "Quiltmaking Basics" for further details as needed.

Quilt assembly

She Who Dares

I made this quilt as a challenge to myself. When I looked at the Arrowhead block, I was immediately drawn to it, but I wasn't sure how to piece it. Once I figured out the math and cutting (thank you, Matt), it turned out to be much easier than I thought. I am delighted with the results. The appearance of a star-within-a-star and the diagonal chain created by the blocks and sashing squares contribute to the overall appeal. No matter what fabrics you choose, it will be a stunning quilt.

Finished Quilt Size: 61" x 74½"
Finished Block Size: 12" x 12" (20 total)

Materials

Yardages are based on 42"-wide fabric unless otherwise noted.

3½ yards of white fabric for blocks, sashing, and border

2⅛ yards of purple fabric for blocks, sashing, and borders

1 yard *total* of assorted colored fabrics for blocks

⅞ yard of horse print or other theme print for blocks and binding*

3¾ yards *or* 1⅞ yards of 108"-wide fabric for backing

65" x 79" piece of batting

*Additional fabric will be required if fussy cutting block centers. Refer to "Determining Yardage for Fussy Cutting" on page 9 for details on estimating yardage.

Cutting

All measurements include ¼"-wide seam allowances.

From the white fabric, cut:

40 strips, 2" x 42"; cut into:

    160 squares, 2" x 2"

    160 rectangles, 2" x 3½"

    49 strips, 2" x 12½"

6 strips, 2½" x 42"; cut into 80 squares, 2½" x 2½"

3 strips, 5" x 42"; cut into 20 squares, 5" x 5"

From the purple fabric, cut:

15 strips, 2" x 42"; cut into 270 squares, 2" x 2"

6 strips, 2⅝" x 42"; cut into 80 squares, 2⅝" x 2⅝"

8 strips, 3" x 42"

From the assorted colored fabrics, cut:

20 squares, 4½" x 4½"

20 squares, 5" x 5"

From the theme print, cut:

20 squares, 3½" x 3½"

8 strips, 2½" x 42"

Assembling the Blocks

1. Sew the 160 white and 160 of the purple 2" squares together into pairs. Press the seam allowances toward the purple squares. Sew the pairs together to make four-patch units as shown; press.

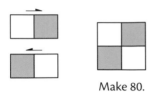

Make 80.

2. Sew 80 white 2" x 3½" rectangles to one side of the four-patch units. Press the seam allowances toward the white rectangles.

3. Sew purple 2" squares to the remaining white 2" x 3½" rectangles. Press the seam allowances toward the white rectangle. Sew the units to the top of the four-patch units as shown; press.

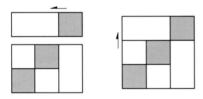

4. Cut the 80 white 2½" squares in half diagonally. Center and sew the wide side of two white triangles to adjacent sides of the purple 2⅝" squares. Press the seam allowances toward the white fabric.

5. Cut the 20 colored 4½" squares twice diagonally. Sew the short side of one of the colored triangles to the upper-right side of 40 of the units from step 4 and 40

to the upper-left side of the units from step 4. Press the seam allowances toward the colored triangles.

Make 40 of each.

6. Referring to "Half-Square-Triangle Units" on page 10 and using the 20 white and 20 colored 5" squares, make 40 half-square-triangle units. Press the seam allowances toward the colored fabric, and then cut in half diagonally across the seam. Don't trim.

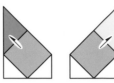

Make 40.   Cut.

7. Sew the pieced triangles to the units from step 5, matching center seams, with the white triangle at the top. Pin carefully to prevent the bias edge from slipping or stretching as you sew. Press, and then carefully trim to 3½" x 5", leaving a ¼" seam allowance beyond the points.

Careful Trimming

It's easy to distort the unit when you trim. I found it worked best to cut the long sides first, and then trim the two shorter sides.

8. Sew the corner units from step 3 to opposite sides of the sections from step 7 as shown. Press the seam allowances toward the corners.

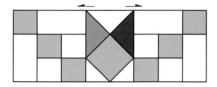

9. Sew the remaining sections from step 7 to opposite sides of the theme print squares. Press the seam allowances toward the center squares.

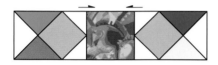

10. Sew the units from step 8 to the top and bottom of the center unit from step 9. Press the seam allowances away from the center sections.

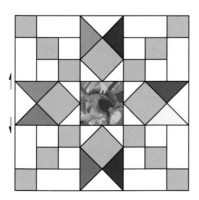

Make 20.

Assembling and Finishing

1. Sew white 2" x 12½" sashing strips to the right sides of all 20 completed blocks. Then sew a white 2" x 12½" sashing strip to the left side of five of the blocks. Press the seam allowances toward the sashing strips.

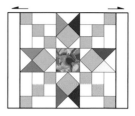

Make 15.   Make 5.

2. Sew five purple 2" squares together with four white 2" x 12½" sashing strips; press toward the white rectangles. Make six sashing rows.

Make 6.

3. Arrange the blocks and sashing rows as shown. Sew the blocks into horizontal rows. Press toward the sashing strips. Sew the rows together; press toward sashing rows.

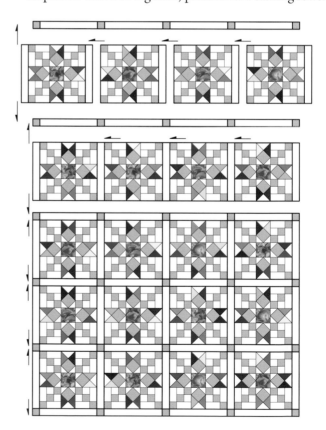

4. Referring to "Borders with Butted Corners" on page 14, measure, cut, and sew the purple 3" border strips to the sides of the quilt; then sew the top and bottom borders.

5. Assemble the quilt sandwich and quilt as desired. Bind the edges using the theme print 2½" strips; add a label. Refer to the finishing techniques beginning on page 16 in "Quiltmaking Basics" for further details as needed.

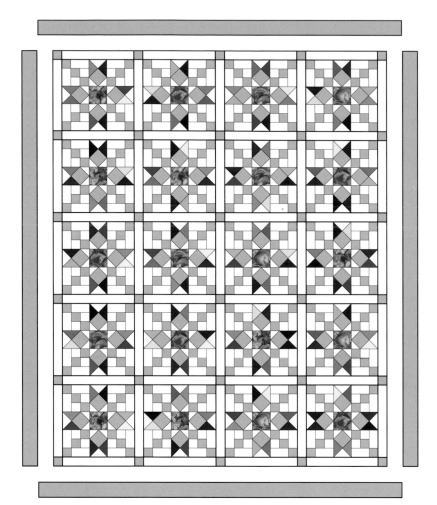

Quilt assembly

A Sunburned Penguin

I've been collecting fabric for a black-and-white quilt for years. There is something about all of the different designs in black-and-white fabric that appeals to me. I finally decided I had to actually make a quilt with those fabrics, and "A Sunburned Penguin" was born. I ended up adding red for contrast, because the block, Domino Net, seemed to work better with three colors. The name of the quilt is actually the punch line to the joke, "What's black and white and red all over?" Don't be afraid to replace the red with another accent color—turquoise, orange, purple, bright pink, or perhaps even yellow.

Finished Quilt Size: 63½" x 72½"
Finished Block Size: 9" x 9" (42 total)

Materials

Yardages are based on 42"-wide fabric unless otherwise noted.

1¾ yards *total* of assorted white with black prints for blocks

1¾ yards *total* of assorted black with white prints for blocks

1⅓ yards of red fabric for blocks and narrow border

⅞ yard of black with white print for outer border

½ yard of white with black print for inner border

⅔ yard of white with black print for binding

3⅞ yards *or* 1⅞ yards of 108"-wide fabric
for backing

68" x 77" piece of batting

Cutting

All measurements include ¼"-wide seam allowances.

From the red fabric, cut:

17 strips, 2" x 42"; cut into 336 squares, 2" x 2"

7 strips, 1" x 42"

From the assorted white with black prints, cut:

252 squares, 2" x 2"

84 squares, 3½" x 3½"

From the assorted black with white prints, cut:

84 squares, 2" x 2"

252 rectangles, 2" x 3½"

From the white with black print for inner border, cut:

7 strips, 2" x 42"

From the black with white print for outer border, cut:

8 strips, 3" x 42"

From the white with black print for binding, cut:

8 strips, 2½" x 42"

Assembling the Blocks

In the steps that follow, *white* refers to white with black prints and *black* refers to black with white prints.

1. Sew 168 red 2" squares to 168 white 2" squares. Press the seam allowances toward the red squares.

Make 168.

2. Sew red 2" squares to the white side of 84 of the units from step 1 and sew black 2" squares to the red side of the remaining 84. Press the seam allowances toward the red fabric.

Make 84 of each.

3. Sew the two different units together, matching seams. Press the seam allowances toward the white/red/black side.

Make 84.

4. Sew the remaining red 2" squares to 84 of the black 2" x 3½" rectangles. Press the seam allowances toward the red squares.

Make 84.

5. Sew the units from step 4 to the white/red/black edge of the units from step 3 as shown. The black rectangle should be next to the black square. Press the seam allowances toward the black/red strips. Set these quarter blocks aside.

6. Sew black 2" x 3½" rectangles to the white 3½" squares. Press the seam allowances toward the black rectangles.

Make 84.

7. Sew the remaining black 2" x 3½" rectangles to the white 2" squares. Press the seam allowances toward the black rectangles.

Make 84.

8. Sew the units from steps 6 and 7 together as shown. Press the seam allowances toward the wider sections.

Make 84.

9. Sew two units from step 8 to two of the completed quarter blocks as shown. Press the seam allowances toward the large white squares. Join the half blocks together to make the blocks; press. Make 42 blocks.

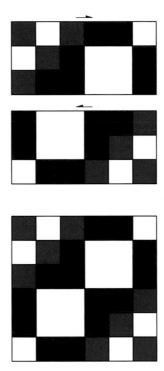

Make 42.

Assembling and Finishing

1. Sew the completed blocks to make 21 pairs. Align the units so that the white sections form a point; press the seam allowances to one side.

2. Sew 18 of the pairs together to make nine large block units with the white fabric forming a diamond. You'll have three pairs of blocks remaining.

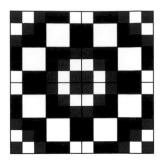

Make 9.

3. Arrange the large blocks and block pairs in rows as shown. Sew the blocks into horizontal rows; then sew the rows together. Press the seam allowances in one direction.

4. Referring to "Borders with Butted Corners" on page 14, measure, cut, and sew the white 2" inner-border strips to the sides of the quilt, and then to the top and bottom. Repeat with the red 1" center-border strips and the black 3" outer-border strips.

Quilt assembly

5. Assemble the quilt sandwich and quilt as desired. Bind the edges using the white 2½" strips; add a label. Refer to the finishing techniques beginning on page 16 in "Quiltmaking Basics" for further details as needed.

Tranquility

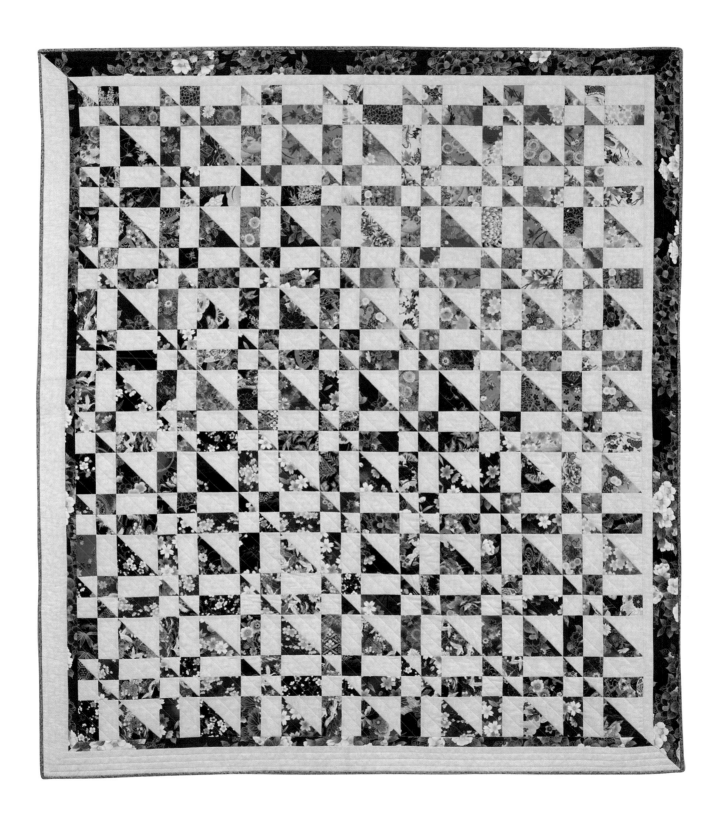

I love the Hopkins Square block because even though perfectly symmetrical, it has the look of being asymmetrical. Careful color placement within the blocks and borders seems to distort reality. I wanted the color to flow from dark to light across the quilt, but I wasn't satisfied with the results until I used a variety of Asian fabrics. I find Asian fabrics to be very beautiful, but I had always thought they should be used in a quilt where their complex designs were highlighted. I discovered that using them in a scrap quilt was a pleasant surprise with exciting results!

Finished Quilt Size: 63½" x 71½"
Finished Block Size: 8" x 8" (56 total)

Materials

Yardages are based on 42"-wide fabric unless otherwise noted.

3¼ yards of ivory fabric for blocks and borders

1⅛ yards *total* of assorted burgundy and red prints for blocks

1⅛ yards *total* of assorted dark purple prints for blocks

1⅛ yards *total* of assorted pink prints for blocks

⅝ yard of dark print for borders

⅔ yard of pink fabric for binding

3⅞ yards *or* 1⅞ yards of 108"-wide fabric the backing

68" x 76" piece of batting

6" Bias Square ruler

Cutting

All measurements include ¼"-wide seam allowances.

From the assorted dark purple prints, cut:

18 squares, 3½" x 3½"

9 squares, 5½" x 5½"

18 squares, 2½" x 2½"

36 rectangles, 2½" x 4½"

From the ivory fabric, cut:

6 strips, 3½" x 42"; cut into 56 squares, 3½" x 3½"

4 strips, 5½" x 42"; cut into 28 squares, 5½" x 5½"

18 strips, 2½" x 42"; cut into:

   56 squares, 2½" x 2½"

   76 rectangles, 2½" x 4½"

4 strips, 1½" x 42"

4 strips, 3" x 42"

From the assorted burgundy and red prints, cut:

20 squares, 3½" x 3½"

10 squares, 5½" x 5½"

20 squares, 2½" x 2½"

40 rectangles, 2½" x 4½"

From the assorted pink prints, cut:

18 squares, 3½" x 3½"

9 squares, 5½" x 5½"

18 squares, 2½" x 2½"

36 rectangles, 2½" x 4½"

From the dark print for borders, cut:

4 strips, 1½" x 42"

4 strips, 3" x 42"

From the pink binding fabric, cut:

8 strips, 2½" x 42"

Assembling the Blocks

1. Referring to "Half-Square-Triangle Units" on page 10 and using the 18 dark purple and 18 ivory 3½" squares, make 36 half-square-triangle units. Press the seam allowances toward the dark fabric. Trim to 2½".

Make 36.

2. In the same manner, make 18 half-square-triangle units using nine dark purple and nine ivory 5½" squares. Press the seam allowances toward the dark fabric and trim to 4½".

3. Sew 15 dark purple 2½" squares to the ivory side of 15 of the small half-square-triangle units and 15 ivory 2½" squares to a dark purple side of 15 of the remaining small half-square-triangle units. Press the seam allowances toward the squares. Set aside the remaining pieces.

Make 15 of each.

4. Sew the 15 half-square-triangle pairs together as shown. The unpieced squares should be in opposite corners, and the triangles should form a diagonal line. Press the seam allowances toward the dark squares.

5. Sew 36 ivory and the 36 dark purple 2½" x 4½" rectangles together into pairs along their long sides. Press the seam allowances toward the dark rectangle.

6. Sew 15 rectangle pairs from step 5 to the side of units from step 4. Press the seam allowances toward the rectangles.

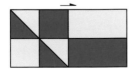

7. Sew the ivory side of 15 of the remaining rectangle pairs to the dark purple side of 15 of the large half-square-triangle units as indicated. Press the seam allowances toward the ivory rectangles. Set aside the remaining pieces.

8. Sew the large and small triangle sets together into blocks; press. The dark triangles should all line up to create a diagonal line through the blocks.

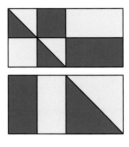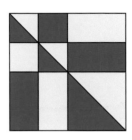

Make 15.

9. Repeat steps 1 through 8 to make 14 burgundy/red blocks and 15 pink blocks. Then, using the set-aside pieces from each group, randomly piece six dark purple and burgundy/red blocks and six burgundy/red and pink transition blocks in the same manner.

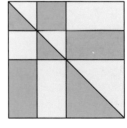

Make 14.   Make 15.

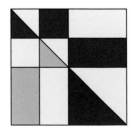

Make 6.   Make 6.

Assembling and Finishing

1. Arrange the blocks in eight rows of seven blocks each with the pink blocks in the upper-right corner and the dark purple blocks in the lower-left corner. Use the transition blocks to blend the sections. Once you are satisfied with the arrangement, sew the blocks into rows; press the seam allowances in opposite directions from row to row. Sew the rows together; press in one direction.

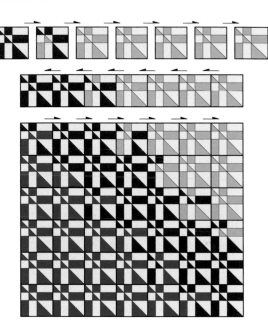

2. Referring to "Borders with Mitered Corners" on page 15, measure, cut, and sew the dark print 1½" inner-border strips to the left side and bottom edge of the quilt and the ivory 1½" border strips to the right side and top edge of the quilt. Repeat for the 3" border strips using ivory for the left side and bottom of the quilt and dark print strips for the right and top edges of the quilt. Press the seam allowances outward.

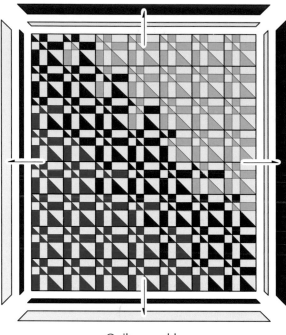

Quilt assembly

3. Assemble the quilt sandwich and quilt as desired. Bind the edges using the pink 2½" strips; add a label. Refer to the finishing techniques beginning on page 16 in "Quiltmaking Basics" for further details as needed.

About the Author

Karin Renaud is a passionate quilter and delights in sharing that passion with others. She enjoys all aspects of quilting, whether it is helping others learn to quilt, making and donating quilts to charity, or making a quilt "just because." No one in her house will ever be too cold! She has been married to her husband, Matt, for nearly 20 years, and they have two amazing children, Luke and Kaitlyn. She lives in Enumclaw, Washington, with her family and three springer spaniels (Beau, Amy and Cal). In addition to quilting, she loves reading, walking, and baseball—especially the Seattle Mariners! She is a lifelong Washingtonian and graduated from Washington State University with a master's degree in speech-language pathology in 1986. Her first book, *Quilts from the Heart* (Martingale & Company), was published in 2006. This is her second book.

Acknowledgments

I owe a debt of thanks to the following people and organizations, without whom this book would not be what it is.

- To Kendall Bledsoe, who painstakingly traced his duck's feet so that I could have a duck print pattern for quilting "Make Way for Ducklings." Who knew that ducks had claws!
- To my cousin Carl and his wife, Heather, who painted their son Kieran's feet to provide the footprints that I used in "The Raspberry Thief."
- To my parents, Diane and Cory Olson, for all of their unconditional love and support.
- To the King County, Washington, Library System for its wonderful collection of audio books. Listening to them made many hours of quilting even more enjoyable.
- To the staff at Martingale & Company, who turn my dreams into tangible books that people can read and enjoy.
- And, last but not least, thank you to my children, Luke and Kaitlyn, for all of your help, feedback, suggestions for quilt names, and for being willing to drive to Portland with me to go fabric shopping. I love you!

New and Best-Selling Titles from

That Patchwork Place®

America's Best-Loved
Quilt Books®

Martingale®
& COMPANY

America's Best-Loved Craft & Hobby Books®
America's Best-Loved Knitting Books®

APPLIQUÉ
Applique Quilt Revival
Beautiful Blooms
Cutting-Garden Quilts
Dream Landscapes—*NEW!*
More Fabulous Flowers
Sunbonnet Sue and Scottie Too

BABIES AND CHILDREN
Baby's First Quilts—*NEW!*
Baby Wraps
Even More Quilts for Baby
Let's Pretend—*NEW!*
The Little Box of Baby Quilts
Snuggle-and-Learn Quilts for Kids
Sweet and Simple Baby Quilts

BEGINNER
Color for the Terrified Quilter
Happy Endings, Revised Edition
Machine Appliqué for the Terrified Quilter
Your First Quilt Book (or it should be!)

GENERAL QUILTMAKING
Adventures in Circles
**American Jane's Quilts for All Seasons—
*NEW!***
Bits and Pieces
Charmed
Cool Girls Quilt
Country-Fresh Quilts—*NEW!*
Creating Your Perfect Quilting Space
Follow-the-Line Quilting Designs Volume
Three
Gathered from the Garden
The New Handmade—*NEW!*
Points of View
Positively Postcards
Prairie Children and Their Quilts
Quilt Revival
A Quilter's Diary
Quilter's Happy Hour
Quilting for Joy—*NEW!*
Sensational Sashiko
Simple Seasons
Skinny Quilts and Table Runners

Twice Quilted
Young at Heart Quilts

HOLIDAY AND SEASONAL
Christmas Quilts from Hopscotch
Christmas with Artful Offerings
Comfort and Joy
Holiday Wrappings

HOOKED RUGS, NEEDLE FELTING,
AND PUNCHNEEDLE
The Americana Collection
Miniature Punchneedle Embroidery
Needle-Felting Magic
Needle Felting with Cotton and Wool
Punchneedle Fun

PAPER PIECING
**Easy Reversible Vests, Revised Edition—
*NEW!***
Paper-Pieced Mini Quilts
Show Me How to Paper Piece
Showstopping Quilts to Foundation Piece
A Year of Paper Piecing

PIECING
501 Rotary-Cut Quilt Blocks—*NEW!*
Better by the Dozen
**Favorite Traditional Quilts Made Easy—
*NEW!***
Loose Change—*NEW!*
Maple Leaf Quilts
Mosaic Picture Quilts
New Cuts for New Quilts
Nine by Nine
On-Point Quilts
Quiltastic Curves
Ribbon Star Quilts
Rolling Along
Sew One and You're Done

QUICK QUILTS
40 Fabulous Quick-Cut Quilts
Instant Bargello
Quilts on the Double
Sew Fun, Sew Colorful Quilts

SCRAP QUILTS
Nickel Quilts
Save the Scraps
Simple Strategies for Scrap Quilts
Spotlight on Scraps

CRAFTS
Art from the Heart
The Beader's Handbook
Card Design
Crochet for Beaders
Dolly Mama Beads
Embellished Memories—*NEW!*
Friendship Bracelets All Grown Up
Making Beautiful Jewelry—*NEW!*
Paper It!—*NEW!*
Sculpted Threads
Sew Sentimental
Trading Card Treasures—*NEW!*

KNITTING & CROCHET
365 Crochet Stitches a Year
365 Knitting Stitches a Year
A to Z of Knitting
All about Knitting—*NEW!*
Amigurumi World
Beyond Wool—*NEW!*
Cable Confidence
Casual, Elegant Knits
Chic Knits
Crocheted Pursenalities
Gigi Knits…and Purls
Kitty Knits
Knitted Finger Puppets—*NEW!*
The Knitter's Book of Finishing
Techniques
Knitting Circles around Socks
Knitting with Gigi
More Sensational Knitted Socks
Pursenalities
Skein for Skein
**Toe-Up Techniques for Hand Knit
Socks, Revised Edition—*NEW!***
Together or Separate—*NEW!*